Cockeyed Education

Cockeyed Education

A Case Method Primer

Gerard Giordano

ROWMAN & LITTLEFIELD EDUCATION

A division of

ROWMAN & LITTLEFIELD PUBLISHERS, INC.
Lanham • New York • Toronto • Plymouth, UK

Published by Rowman & Littlefield Education
A division of Rowman & Littlefield Publishers, Inc.
A wholly owned subsidary of The Rowman & Littlefield Publishing Group, Inc.
4501 Forbes Boulevard, Suite 200, Lanham, Maryland 20706
http://www.rowmaneducation.com

Estover Road
Plymouth PL6 7PY
United Kingdom

British Library Cataloguing in Publication Information Available

Library of Congress Cataloging-in-Publication Data

Giordano, Gerard.
    Cockeyed education : a case method primer / Gerard Giordano.
      p. cm.
    Includes bibliographical references.
    ISBN 978-1-60709-434-0 (cloth : alk. paper) — ISBN 978-1-60709-435-7 (pbk. : alk. paper) — ISBN 978-1-60709-436-4 (electronic)
    1. Case method. 2. Education—United States—History. 3. Education—United States—Case studies. 4. Problem solving. I. Title.
    LC1029.C37G56 2010
    371.39—dc22   2009031963

Printed in the United States of America

♾ ™ The paper used in this publication meets the minimum requirements of American National Standard for Information Sciences—Permanence of Paper for Printed Library Materials, ANSI/NISO Z39.48-1992.

This book is for my collaborators and coauthors—
my students.

Table of Contents

Preface

Cockeyed Education

I sure had some cockeyed ideas

—Humphrey Bogart, 1948 [From the film *Treasure of the Sierra Madre*; quoted by Huston & Traven, 1979.]

This book looks at recommendations for the schools. It examines recommendations from two groups: persons involved directly with them and those associated indirectly.

The persons who are involved directly include teachers, school administrators, and numerous other professionals. The persons who associate with the schools indirectly include parents, businesspersons, military leaders, and politicians. They also include scholars: educational researchers, philosophers, psychologists, sociologists, political scientists, anthropologists, economists, marketers, physical therapists, animal therapists, journalists, architects, health care professionals, and even specialists on popular culture.

This book examines race, religion, ethnicity, gender, poverty, and other issues that are critical to the schools. It also examines issues that are less important, but still relevant. These issues include video games, school facilities, classroom discipline, and standardized tests.

This book, which is an introduction to the case method, provides the basis for group discussions. However, it contains activities that enable a single reader to simulate participation in these discussions. It is aimed at parents, educators, and community leaders; it is designed to help them differentiate sound advice from cockeyed advice.

Acknowledgement

It is difficult for me to find the right words with which to thank my extraordinary editor, Tom Koerner. Were it not for Tom's encouragement, confidence, and vision, this book would not have been written.

List of Tables

Chapter 1

Is the Case Method Similar to Gonzo Journalism?

What I would like to preserve here is a kind of high-speed cinematic reel-record of what the campaign was like at the time, not what the whole thing boiled down to or how it fits into history.

—Hunter Thompson, 1973

Some persons used the case method to excite students. Others used it to help them solve taxing problems.

THE CASE METHOD

The case method is a question-based approach to teaching and learning. Although it struck some people as simple, enthusiasts had a difficult time agreeing about it. They even had difficulty agreeing about a name. They alternately referred to it as the case study method, the case history method, the case study method of instruction, the case study method of learning, and the case study method of problem solving. Some referred to it by its historical name, the Socratic Method.

In addition to disagreeing about a name for the case method, enthusiasts disagreed about how they should describe it. Worried that concise, encyclopedia-like descriptions would misrepresent the process, they preferred to explain it with circuitous strategies, such as those in the following passages.

Politicians

During the 2008 presidential campaign, Senator Hillary Clinton was competing for her party's presidential nomination. She wished to demonstrate that she had the experiences and the character of an effective commander in chief. Therefore she referred to an incident from the era when she had been First Lady.

Senator Clinton recalled landing on a Bosnian airfield that was under attack. She indicated that she had remained poised as she dodged deadly sniper fire. She claimed that her demeanor revealed that she had the resolution, grit, courage, and preparation to serve as commander in chief.

Political opponents challenged Senator Clinton's recollections. They pointed out that a cheerful entourage, which had included professional entertainers and her own daughter, had joined her on that airstrip. They noted that none of these persons recalled the attack. They added that the journalists accompanying the senator had not mentioned the attack in their reports. They eventually located video recordings to dispute the senator's recollections (Seelye, 2008).

Clinton's opponents were not finished; they had additional machinations in mind. They located a photo of the senator making a military-style salute, printed the phrase "pusillanimous warrior" beneath it, and circulated it on the Internet.

When I saw the irreverent photo, I was struck by the word *pusillanimous*. Although I realized that the adjective had been selected to mock Senator Clinton, I was not sure of its definition. This was not my first encounter with this adjective. During the early 1970s, a Republican vice president had created a political raucous when he labeled his political opponents as "pusillanimous pussyfooters." Reporters delighted in repeating this phrase (Clines, 1996).

Editorialists

The adjective *pusillanimous* resurfaced on several other occasions. For example, an editorial writer claimed that conservative Christians were annoyed at preachers who were ignoring those Biblical passages that they found personally discomforting. This author denigrated these clergy as "pusillanimous pastors" ("Pusillanimous Pastors Are Worse," 2007).

Another author caught my attention in a highly editorialized book. He recounted that he repeatedly had pleaded with congressional representatives to impeach President George W. Bush. Upset that they had not taken his advice, he dismissed them as "pusillanimous legislators" (Nichols, 2006).

Clients at Dating Services

The adjective *pusillanimous* showed up still again while I was conversing with a colleague. This colleague, who was a widower, was interested in meeting companions through a computer-based dating service. He filled out questionnaires so that the service could match him with suitable partners. He then contacted the individuals to whom he was referred.

My colleague was about to give up on the dating service after he was not attracted to any of the persons with whom he had been matched. However, he realized that his luck had changed after he was connected to an individual who was witty, compassionate, empathetic, vibrant, and charismatic. This person shared his taste in music, art, literature, films, and politics. Nonetheless, the person declined to get together with him.

After my friend summoned the courage to ask his correspondent whether they ever would meet, he became disconsolate. The person wished to terminate their relationship. My friend begged to know the reason.

The person responded that my friend's personality profile revealed that he was cautious, hesitant, shy, and pusillanimous. This person had been involved with several individuals who had these traits, had been disappointed in them, and had no intention of dating another inappropriate person.

When my friend related these incidents to me, he enunciated each of the four labels that his correspondent had attached to him. Upset and confused, he asked me whether I thought that he was cautious, hesitant, shy, and pusillanimous. Before I could answer, he looked at me and asked, "What exactly does *pusillanimous* mean?"

I responded slowly. I told him that I had encountered this word on several occasions. Refining my impression after each encounter, I concluded that *pusillanimous* was similar to *cautious, hesitant,* and *shy*—the other three adjectives that his correspondent had hurled at him. I thought that the term also might mean cowardly; however, I concealed this last hunch from my friend.

JOURNALISTS

Hunter Thompson assembled a memorable account of Richard Nixon's 1970s reelection campaign. He wrote in detail about George McGovern's futile attempts to make that important political contest competitive. However, Thompson did not follow the prevalent style of reporting. Using an approach that he called gonzo journalism, he wrote about political incidents in which he was involved. In fact, he portrayed himself as a participant in those incidents (Thompson, 1973).

Thompson made no pretense of writing objectively; he did not suppress his preconceptions, values, and personal attitudes. Employing a first-person style of writing, he was frequently abrasive and always irreverent. He alienated some readers while attracting others.

Thompson's reporting style had benefits for him as a writer. It enabled him to convey insights with vibrancy, unity, coherence, and wit. It also had benefits for his readers. It stimulated them, provided them with a narrative skeleton, and gave them chances to discern similarities between the incidents about which they were reading and those in which they personally were involved.

Enthusiasts of gonzo journalism claimed that this technique affected persons who were consuming information as well as those who were conveying it. The enthusiasts of the case method made similar claims about their technique.

LAWYERS

The early professors of law wished to prepare their students for the legal profession; they required them to memorize statutes, ordinances, restrictions, and precedents. They hoped that encyclopedic knowledge would enable the students to pass bar exams; they hoped that it would enable them to establish prosperous professional practices.

Professors at Harvard University were dissatisfied with the memorization-based approach that their students were using. They noted that students were attempting to retain a body of information that already was unwieldy. Ready for a change in learning techniques, they advised their students to analyze rather than memorize information; they advised them to use the case method.

When the law students began to use the case method, they focused on written decisions from critical court cases. They analyzed the logic that had guided the judges who had penned those decisions. They then extrapolated their insights from historical to current incidents (Ashley, 1990; Barton, 2008; Erskine, Leenders, & Mauffette-Leenders, 1998).

Although the law professors retired the memorization-based approach to instruction, they retained many of the pedagogical practices with which they had been supplementing it. For example, they had required students to study individually; they continued to encourage them to learn in this manner.

After they had transitioned to the case method, the law professors required their students to orally reprise and analyze the details of legal cases. Even though they made the students recite information, they did not grade these responses. They continued to assign grades exclusively on the basis of written exams.

After experimenting with the case method, the Harvard professors were excited about it. Professors and students at other law schools were equally excited. Within two decades, they were following the Harvard pedagogical procedures.

BUSINESSPERSONS

Professors at Harvard's law school had been looking for a more effective instructional approach; they experimented with the case method during the 1890s. They made an impression on the business professors, who also were looking for a different type of pedagogy. Several decades after the law professors had implemented the case method, the Harvard business professors tried it.

The business professors adapted the case method for their peculiar situation. Because they wished to enhance students' practical knowledge about commercial, industrial, financial, and entrepreneurial practices, they asked them to read and analyze synopses of business incidents. Because they did not have access to documents written by the participants in those incidents, they personally wrote their own synopses.

The business professors were aware that the lawyers rarely supplemented legal decisions with other types of materials. Nonetheless, they decided to provide students with extensive supplementary materials: financial statements, stock reports, marketing materials, strategic plans, board minutes, newspaper stories, and testimonials from persons who had witnessed incidents (Garvin, 2000).

The business professors made additional changes to the case method. Instead of requiring students to study on their own, they encouraged them to study in groups. They hoped that this practice would foster collaboration and communication. They then assigned grades on the basis of their group efforts (Jain, 2008; McDonald & Milne, 1999; Randrup & Sekits, 2007).

EDUCATORS

Professors in law and business realized that their students had to encapsulate, comprehend, and use limitless amounts of information. They did not want them to memorize information; they wanted them to use it as competent practitioners would use it.

Professors of education were aware that their own students had to learn vast amounts of information. Some of them had tried to help by limiting the information for which they were responsible. They parsed information into two categories: the information that scientific researchers had endorsed and that which they had not endorsed. They then encouraged the students to pay attention only to the researcher-endorsed information. However, they were confronted by critics.

Difficulties

Critics asked whether the biases of educational researchers had reduced the value of their observations and recommendations. They found multiple examples to underscore their concerns. For example, they pointed to biases and conflicts of interest among late twentieth-century reading researchers; they focused intently on personnel in California's department of education (Giordano, 2004, 2009).

During the 1980s and 1990s, the California education leaders had the authority to direct the types of reading instruction, materials, and assessments that the teachers in their state employed. Aware of the controversy surrounding these issues, they traditionally had allowed school administrators to use their discretion. However, they decided to change their approach.

The California leaders gave their teachers a directive: rely exclusively on holistic, language-based instruction, learning materials, and assessments. They required teachers to substitute children's literature books for basal reading textbooks, informal styles of teaching for structured approaches, and informal assessments for standardized tests.

The proponents of the holistic approach were able to rationalize their restrictions. They pointed out that this instruction made sense in California, where many students spoke English as their second language. They explained that this instruction could be readily adapted for these learners. They added that holistic learning materials and holistic assessments also made sense because they complemented the pedagogical objectives of holistic instruction.

Some Californians did not accept the rationale for holistic reading instruction; they were not eager to implement it. Teachers who had been successful with other types of instruction challenged the initiative. They questioned the wisdom of requiring a single pedagogical approach. They were joined by skeptical parents. Many of these parents had children who had tried holistic instruction and failed with it.

The critics also questioned the observations that had been used to validate holistic instruction. They identified biases and conflicts of interests among the teachers who had embraced holistic instruction, the researchers who had investigated it, and the state bureaucrats who had prescribed it.

The critics demanded that their state educational leaders objectively assess holistic instruction; they demanded that they reinstate standardized reading tests. They warned them that these tests would show declines from earlier scores. As it became clear that the warnings were accurate, the public joined the uproar about reading education in California (Giordano, 2000, 2009).

Californians wrangled about numerous educational issues. When the members of a faction attempted to resolve disagreements with scientific research, they could not find conclusive studies. Some of them requested additional time to conduct more studies. Others gave up on scientific research and turned to populist advice.

Observers were upset when the residents in numerous states expressed frustrations similar to those of the Californians. Some of them were dismayed by their attitudes toward scientific and populist advice. Having concluded that the factions were behaving in cockeyed manners, they turned to a distinct style of problem solving: the case method.

Adaptations

When educators resolved to use the case method, they could have followed law or business professors. The educators realized that these groups had implemented the case method differently. The law professors analyzed decisions that judges had written; the business professors analyzed synopses that they had written.

The educators discerned other differences between the business and law professors. They noted that the business professors gave students extensive supplementary materials, organized them into small teams, and used their group interactions to calculate grades.

When professors of education used the case method, they decided that they would make a predictable adaptation: they would focus on educational incidents. However, they still had to make decisions about pedagogical practices.

The education professors were impressed with the ways in which the business professors had written synopses of incidents, built teams, encouraged collaboration, and used a multitask style of grading. They resolved to incorporate these practices into their own courses (Brookfield & Preskill, 1999; Colbert, Desberg, & Trimble, 1996; Herreid, 2007; Mennin, Schwartz, & Webb, 2001).

The education professors admired another practice of the business professors: the way in which business professors supplemented their synopses of incidents with additional relevant information. Education professors decided to supplement their own synopses with information about the social, cultural, political, and economic conditions affecting the schools (Giordano, 2009).

EXAMINING ADVICE ABOUT THE CASE METHOD

Students were eager to try the case method. They were excited because it enabled them to organize information, retain it, form insights, and apply those insights to other situations. Many of them remained enthusiastic after they tried it.

Even though some students were excited about the case method, others were disconcerted. The malcontents were bothered by the ways in which session leaders conducted meetings or classes. They were upset when they posed problems and asked for answers, but then refused to reveal whether answers were correct. They concluded that their leaders were eccentric and that the case method was frustrating.

In this chapter, you have reviewed several approaches to the case method. Additionally, you have evaluated these approaches. You even used case-method strategies in your evaluations. However, you still may wish to use the case method in the way that you would in a discussion group. In this type of situation, you would interact with a skilled session leader and with other participants.

The following activities involve questions similar to those that session leaders would pose during case-based discussions. Although they do not duplicate discussions, they reveal the ways in which leaders might steer them. If you complete these activities with other readers, you can collaborate with them on the responses.

Activity 1.1

You might wish to examine the case method and another unconventional technique for analyzing information. You could use Table 1.1.

Table 1.1 lists two analytical techniques: gonzo journalism and the case method. It gives you opportunities to identify a salient characteristic of each technique. It also gives you opportunities to identify an advantage and a disadvantage for each.

Table 1.1. Analytical Techniques

Technique	Characteristic	Advantage	Disadvantage
Gonzo Journalism			
Case Method			

Activity 1.2

You could examine the case method from another perspective. You could examine the ways in which it is employed within distinct professional schools. You could use Table 1.2.

Table 1.2 asks you to identify a salient characteristic of the case method as it is practiced in schools of law. It also asks you to identify a characteristic of the case method as it is practiced in schools of business. To complete the table, specify an advantage and disadvantage of each.

Table 1.2.   Two Instances of the Case Method

Case Method	Characteristic	Advantage	Disadvantage
Law			
Business			

Activity 1.3

You might wish to examine the case method from still another perspective. You could compare the distinctive ways in which it has been adapted. You could use Table 1.3.

Table 1.3 lists three groups: lawyers, businesspersons, and educators. It gives you chances to identify the ways in which these groups have adapted the case method. It also gives you opportunities to specify the advantages and disadvantages of their adaptations. To complete this table, you could rely on the information in this chapter, the books that are cited in it, additional books, or your personal experiences.

Table 1.3.   Three Instances of the Case Method

Case Method	Characteristic	Advantage	Disadvantage
Law			
Business			
Education			

SUMMARY

Some educators viewed the case method as a tool with which to guide discussions. They helped students analyze incidents and form insights about them. Other educators viewed the case method as a tool with which to solve practical problems. They helped students analyze incidents, form insights, and generalize their insights to novel situations.

Chapter 2

Can Students Learn With Video Games?

Donkey Kong. . . . [from] the early 1980s. . . . was voted the third best coin-operated arcade video game of all time. . . . and grown men still pursue each other across the country in pursuit of the world-record Donkey Kong score.

—Roger Ebert, 2007

Most persons acknowledged that video games were entertaining. However, enthusiasts claimed that they stimulated learning and prepared players to solve real-world problems. Critics disagreed vehemently.

CONTROVERSIAL GAMES

Young males loved to fantasize. They were attracted to adventure-themed novels, movies, and comic books. They later were drawn to adventure-themed videogames such as *World of Warcraft, Grand Theft Auto, Metal Gear Solid, Legend of Zelda, Resident Evil, Chrono Trigger, Final Fantasy, Dragon Warrior,* and *Half-Life.*

Although they prized adventure-themed videogames, young males were interested in other genres as well. They eagerly played basketball, baseball, football, soccer, tennis, billiards, and bowling games. They loved games in which they navigated cars, motorcycles, go-karts, skateboards, surfboards, or snowboards. They relished wrestling, boxing, karate, and street-fighting games. They savored puzzle, role-playing, and novelty games.

Growth of Gaming

During the first half of the twentieth century, savvy marketers had predicted that young males would be a critical audience for movies and comic books. Decades later, they predicted that they would be the primary purchasers of video games (Cassell & Jenkins, 2000). In both instances, they verified their forecasts with sales.

Video games are immensely profitable. They generated over twenty billion dollars in the United States during 2007. They increased that amount by twenty percent during the following year. *Grand Theft Auto,* which was introduced in 1997, sold more than seventy million copies over the next ten years (Schiesel, 2008b, 2009).

Although video games attract numerous male customers, they also attract significant numbers of females. In one survey, females between twelve and seventeen years of age were asked about the frequency with which they played videogames. More than ninety percent indicated that they played them regularly (Lenhart, Kahne, Middaugh, Macgill, Evans, & Vitak, 2008).

Some video games, such as *The Sims,* attract many females. This game provides opportunities for the players to select characters and then steer them through social situations. In the 2009 edition of *The Sims,* players can designate the physical appearances of their characters; however, they also can pick the ways in which they behave and even the ways in which they make decisions.

The Sims games have been translated into multiple languages and marketed in dozens of countries. Earning more than four billion dollars by 2008, they became the bestselling video games of all time (Clifford, 2009; Schiesel, 2008a).

Persons view video games from multiple perspectives. They hold different opinions about whether the games are relaxing, competitive, personal, social, intellectual, or emotional. They also have different opinions about the value of the games (Gee, 2004, 2007; Johnson, 2006; Palfrey & Gasser, 2008; Prensky, 2006, 2007; Shaffer, 2006).

Praise

Educators who appreciated the entertainment value of video games were pleased when they observed students playing them. Some of them valued the practical benefits of the games.

Enthusiastic educators were sure that video game playing developed technology skills. They hoped that players would transfer those skills to other situations, acquire vocational training, or procure employment in technical occupations. Even though they believed that video games had practical benefits, they suspected that they also had intellectual and emotional benefits.

Criticism

Angry critics condemned videogames. They worried that children and adolescents who played them would lose interest in athletic and social activities. They feared that they might lose interest in classroom activities.

Critics had additional reasons for discouraging children from playing video games. They pointed out that some characters in video games were materialistic, violent, and sexually promiscuous; they warned that the children who played the games would model these behaviors (Anderson, Gentile, & Buckley, 2007; Kutner & Olson, 2008).

CONTROVERSIAL INSTRUCTION

Critics raised questions about the ways in which video games influenced children. This was not the first time that they had doubts about the ways in which novel media and learning materials affected children. Early critics were skeptical about numerous types of materials, including those that had been designed explicitly for instruction.

Early Anxiety

At the beginning of the twentieth century, parents were anxious when their children struggled in school; they were particularly anxious when they did not learn to read. They recognized that this failure had disturbing consequences.

Parents worried that children who failed in reading would fail in other academic areas. They also worried that they would face problems after they had left school; they worried that they would have difficulties with employment, social status, and even emotional health. They felt that they had good reasons to be upset.

Although parents were upset about children who had not learned to read, they also were perplexed. They pointed out that some of them seemed to have as much mental aptitude as the children who became readers. After they had listened to the responses from teachers and school administrators, they still were disappointed; in fact, they were disappointed because of their responses.

Although the teachers and school administrators cared about children who had not learned to read, they did not know how to help them. They proposed to retain them in their current grades and give them additional opportunities to master the reading curriculum.

Parents were not excited about proposals to delay children in school. They pointed out that most of the children who had been held back had not learned to read. Disappointed by the educators, they went to physicians.

After examining the children, the physicians had good news: the children were neither lazy nor stupid. They concluded that they were unable to read because they had peculiar disabilities. In addition to being sympathetic and insightful, the physicians were entrepreneurial. They resolved that they would establish private clinics at which to treat children with reading disabilities.

Distinctive Therapy

Although physicians believed that physical irregularities caused reading problems, they were not sure about the precise details. Some of them hypothesized that the irregularities were neurological; others hypothesized that they were sensory.

One group of physicians conjectured that irregular eye movements affected reading; they offered to establish clinics at which to diagnose children. Although the parents did want the physicians to diagnose children, they also wanted them to help them. The physicians initially replied that they did not have the time, skills, or inclination to correct learning problems. However, they eventually compromised: they hired experienced teachers to instruct the children.

After they had hired teachers, physicians hired another group of professionals—businesspersons. They asked the businesspersons to manage and advertise their clinics. The businesspersons were keyed up about these opportunities. They recruited clients, informed them about the etiologies of reading problems, and convinced them that the doctors could help (Giordano, 2000).

Parents of children with severe reading problems were excited about the learning clinics; they viewed them as places at which their children would be able to catch up with their peers. Even the parents of normally progressing and gifted children were excited; they viewed the clinics as places where their children could maintain their leads over peers or get further ahead of them.

Although the private learning clinics offered opportunities, they had limitations. Because they were situated in large cities, they excluded many rural residents. Because they were private, they excluded persons who could not afford them.

Distinctive Machines

Physicians asked businesspersons to help them establish private clinics, advertise them, recruit clients, and manage their operations. They presented them with an additional challenge: they asked them to devise equipment to diagnose reading problems.

The businesspersons again responded eagerly. They were sure that they could design machines with which to observe and photograph eye movements; they thought that they could adapt these machines to correct inappropriate eye movements. Although they initially developed mechanical devices, they eventually devised electronic equipment (Giordano, 2000).

The businesspersons fashioned special projectors to display passages in rhythmic patterns. These projectors were essentially electronic textbooks. Proponents were sure that they would eliminate learning problems. However, critics were skeptical.

Critics were concerned about the research studies that the eye-movement enthusiasts had conducted; they complained that they could not replicate them. They also complained about the electronic textbooks, which they characterized as expensive, cumbersome, and unreliable gadgets.

Enthusiasts ignored their critics and continued to employ electronic textbooks. After personal computers became available, they used them to regulate eye movements, change the formats of texts, embed animation into learning activities, maintain records of students' progress, and integrate comprehension and vocabulary drills into lessons (Giordano, 2000).

CONTROVERSIAL LEARNING MATERIALS

The very early teachers had insisted that students learn to read with religious materials or classic works of literature. Later instructors, who detected the limitations of these materials, preferred textbooks that were designed specifically for reading.

Because they were unable to teach many children to read with religious books, works of literature, or textbooks, instructors continued to search for the ideal learning materials. Some of them eventually turned to popular fiction. Pleased with the enthusiasm for these books, they hoped that students would transfer their excitement to other types of books. However, they had to deal with critics.

Critics denigrated popular books with terms such as "newsstand novels," "dime-store detectives," and "drug-store romances." They warned that they would lead to vulgarity, liberal sexual attitudes, juvenile delinquency, and violence. They searched for political allies.

Comic Books

The group that opposed popular fiction in the schools was joined by another faction: that which opposed comic books. The critics of comic books worried that these materials would distract students from academic learning. However, they had much graver worries.

In a widely read book, Frederick Wertham (1954) warned that comics exposed children to acts of crime and deviance. He insisted that they would persuade readers to commit similar acts. He revealed his alarmist attitudes in his book's title—*Seduction of the Innocent.*

Wertham advised parents, educators, and government leaders that comic books had highly erotic themes. He used the Batman series as an example. He asserted that readers would have to employ little imagination to recognize the homosexual symbols in books where the protagonist was a social outcast, lived with a young male, wore physically provocative costumes, resided in a cave, and entered the cave in a torpedo-like car.

Politicians joined the uproar over comic books. They particularly worried that these books might cause juvenile delinquency (United States Senate Committee on the Judiciary, 1954). During the 1950s, they arranged congressional hearings to explore and publicize this link. Their interest increased when they detected signs that the national anti-comics stir might expand to other countries (Lent, 1999).

Although the opponents and the supporters of comic books clashed repeatedly, they eventually agreed to cooperate by forming a censorship board. They directed the members of the board to devise a code to identify damaging materials, such as those that depicted illicit, abnormal, or perverse sex (Nyberg, 1998).

Therapeutic Books

As textbook authors and publishers became more sophisticated, they created materials that were filled with innovative drills, charts, tables, and diagrams. Their materials no longer resembled the books that persons handled outside of the schools.

Although some educators prized pedagogically sophisticated textbooks, others were upset. The critics worried that the textbooks had become so unnatural that they could inhibit learning. They recommended that teachers return to traditional books (Giordano, 2003).

The textbook critics were especially censorious of reading textbooks. They pointed out these books used unnatural language patterns and meaningless stories to help children master phonics and other word-identification skills. Questioning the value of these skills, they encouraged teachers to use a children's literature approach.

The proponents of the children's literature approach directed students to stimulating sentences, interesting passages, and enticing stories. They predicted that the students who were exposed to children's books would not only learn classroom skills but also transfer them to other books, magazines, and the printed information outside of their classrooms (Giordano, 2000).

Some teachers were not satisfied after they had surrounded students with books. They hoped to locate materials that were extraordinarily suitable for them. They employed bibliotherapy, an instructional approach that required them to diagnose students' emotional problems (Giordano, 2000, 2009).

After they had determined their students' emotional problems, teachers selected books or stories in which the characters were confronting similar problems. They predicted that the students, who would be highly attracted to the materials, would learn to read more easily than they would with textbooks (Cornett & Cornett, 1980; Haldeman & Idstein, 1977).

Some of the instructors who used bibliotherapy attempted to simplify the approach. Instead of selecting materials that matched the problems of individual students, they selected materials that corresponded to the problems that most children experienced (Rubin, 1978). Instructors who were teaching young students selected books about strangers, the dark, or separation from parents. Instructors who were teaching older students selected books about peer relationships, careers, or weight gain.

Although some instructors relied on materials that were not developed specifically for students with emotional problems, others used commercial materials that were designed for special audiences. Instructors could discern the audiences for which commercial books were intended simply by examining their titles: *Shelley, the Hyperactive Turtle; Cory Stories—A Kid's Book About Living With ADHD;* or *Otto Learns About His Medicine—A Story About Medication for Hyperactive Children* (Galvin & Ferraro, 1988; Kraus & Martin, 2005; Moss & Schwartz, 1989).

Instead of prescribing or even recommending books for their students, instructors sometimes surrounded them with heterogeneous materials. After encouraging them to make selections, they used those materials to individualize reading lessons (e.g. Fader & McNeil, 1968).

Some educators and parents criticized bibliotherapy. They were worried that students would select books that would not enable their teachers to implement rigorous academic curricula. They also had concerns about teachers. They worried that some of them lacked the time or the talent to implement individualized lessons.

Critics had other reasons for distrusting bibliotherapy. They questioned whether teachers had the training and sensitivity to recognize emotional problems. They worried that they might exacerbate or even create emotional problems. They concluded that bibliotherapy could not compete with the basal-reading programs.

Dialect Books

Twentieth-century educators worried about children who spoke languages other than English. They reasoned that learning to read, which was difficult enough by itself, became more difficult when children had to decipher vocabulary and grammar from a second language. They looked for a way to simplify their learning.

School reformers pressed for extensive changes in reading instruction during the 1960s. Concerned about the many immigrant children who spoke languages other than English, they began to offer instruction in the children's native languages. Although they focused initially on children who were bilingual, they eventually extended their efforts to another group—children who spoke nonstandard dialects.

The reformers argued that children who spoke dialects other than Standard English were in positions similar to bilingual children. They urged the teachers of these children to use materials that had been "translated" into dialects (Giordano, 2000). Because they focused almost exclusively on teaching reading to African American children, they referred to the dialect-based materials as "black readers."

When the reformers converted reading materials into a nonstandard African American dialect, they assumed that minority parents would approve. They were surprised when the parents objected. The parents objected for a political reason: they linked the materials to racial segregation. They explained that the use of dialect readers required the separation of minority children from their non-minority peers.

Parents also objected to dialect readers for practical reasons. The materials were based on a dialect spoken by the African American children in a New York neighborhood. Because the materials employed a distinctive geographical dialect, they were not ideally suited to children who lived in other areas. Because the dialect on which they were based was changing rapidly, the materials quickly became obsolete.

The 1960s advocates of dialect readers had assumed that African American parents would be enthusiastic. They were surprised when they raised political and practical objections. After they realized that the African American parents were not supportive, the enthusiasts stopped promoting the materials.

When the dialect readers were introduced in the 1960s, they were not particularly eventful. When they were reintroduced during the 1990s, they created a tumult. In fact, they created a national and international commotion.

The 1990s advocates of dialect readers relied on the same arguments as earlier enthusiasts (Baugh, 2000; Leland & Joseph, 1997; Perry & Delpit, 1998; Ramirez, 2005). However, they chose a new name for the learning materials; they referred to them as Ebonics materials. As had been the case decades earlier, they had to deal with critics.

Journalist and political commentators posed questions about the Ebonics learning materials. When they were not satisfied with the answers from the enthusiasts, they wrote caustic commentaries. They were joined by African American parents, who concluded that the political and practical disadvantages of the materials outweighed their pedagogical advantages.

Novel Media

Novel media emerged throughout the twentieth century. Some of them, such as eye-movement projectors, were designed specifically for education. However, others, such as films, radios, phonographs, tape recorders, televisions, video recorders, and computers, were designed for business and entertainment. All of these media were introduced into the schools.

Supporters claimed that novel learning materials stimulated learners and prepared them to interact with media outside of their classrooms. They claimed that they prepared them for special careers. They claimed that they fostered cognitive, social, physical, and emotional learning. However, they had to respond to critics.

Critics dismissed the claims of the enthusiasts. They characterized the novel media as expensive paraphernalia for entertaining rather than instructing students. They worried that they diverted and possibly alienated students from textbooks and other printed materials.

The early critics warned that novel media had especially destructive consequences when they were infused with popular culture. Later critics repeated these cautions. They warned that students would access sensual music through CDs, record inappropriate acts with digital cameras, and view sexually explicit materials on the Internet.

EXAMINING ADVICE ABOUT LEARNING MATERIALS

When enthusiasts introduced novel learning materials into the schools, they assured teachers that they were beneficial. However, opponents challenged this assertion.

Activity 2.1

You might wish to examine novel materials. You could examine the debates about them in the schools. You could use Table 2.1.

Table 2.1 lists five types of learning materials: reading machines, books used during bibliotherapy, comic books, dialect materials, and video games. If you wished to add other materials to this list, you might select phonograph records, radio programs, films, tape recordings, television programs, or video recordings. You could add materials by yourself, with another reader, or with a small group of readers.

To complete this table, identify a strength and weakness for each type of learning material. As a final step, explain your comments.

Table 2.1.   Educational Materials

Material	Strength	Weakness	Explanation
Reading Machine			
Bibliotherapy			
Comic Book			
Dialect Reader			
Video Game			

Activity 2.2

You could choose another perspective from which to examine novel learning materials. You could identify the ways in which groups reacted when these materials were introduced into the schools. You could rely on Table 2.2.

Table 2.2 lists five types of learning materials: reading machines, books used during bibliotherapy, comic books, dialect readers, and video games. It also identifies five groups of educational stakeholders: parents, teachers, principals, politically conservative school board members, and politically liberal school board members.

Use symbols to complete this table. Use the symbol – if the members of a group expressed low support for learning materials. Use the symbol –/+ for moderate support and the symbol + for high support. Finally, explain your selections. You can complete this table by yourself, with another reader, or with a small group of readers.

Table 2.2. Reactions to Educational Materials

Group	Material*					Explanation
	Reading Machine	Biblio-therapy	Comic Book	Dialect Reader	Video Game	
Parents						
Teachers						
Principals						
Politically Conservative School Boards						
Politically Liberal School Boards						

* (–) Low Support
(–/+) Moderate Support
(+) High Support

Activity 2.3

You could choose still another perspective from which to examine novel learning materials. You might wish to concentrate on the different ways that critics reacted to them. You could employ Table 2.3.

Table 2.3 identifies five types of learning materials: reading machines, books used in bibliotherapy, comic books, dialect readers, and video games. It provides you with the opportunities to indicate the ways in which critics reacted to the distinctive format of each material. It also gives you chances to indicate their reactions to the content.

Use numerals to complete this table. Use the numeral *1* if critics expressed mild criticism. Use the numeral *2* for moderate criticism and the numeral *3* for intense criticism. Finally, explain the basis for the scores that you selected. You could rely on the information in this chapter, the books that are cited in it, additional books, or your personal experiences.

Table 2.3. Criticizing Educational Materials

Material	*Criticism**		*Explanation*
	Format	*Content*	
Reading Machine			
Bibliotherapy			
Comic Book			
Dialect Reader			
Video Game			

* (1) Mild
  (2) Moderate
  (3) Intense

SUMMARY

Some educators valued comic books, magazines, films, televisions programs, and video games. They claimed that they stimulated students' interest, accelerated their learning, enabled them to solve practical problems, and prepared them for special careers. However, they were challenged by critics.

The critics worried that the format of novel learning materials reduced students' enthusiasm for traditional classroom materials. They also worried that the content could damage them morally and emotionally.

Chapter 3

Should Students be Paid to Learn?

Psychologists have warned against giving children prizes or money for their performance in school. . . . but many economists and businesspeople disagree."

—Lisa Guernsey, 2009

The early teachers relied on fear to motivate students. However, they eventually experimented with other incentives.

COMMERCIALIZATION

Teachers and community members continually attempted to find effective ways to motivate students. Some of them came up with a novel suggestion: they wished to prod them with money. Even though they explained that this suggestion was experimental, they were challenged by irate critics.

Critics had practical question about paying students to learn. They immediately wanted to know the sources of the payments. The enthusiasts had a ready answer: philanthropists would fund their experiments. However, the critics raised other types of questions.

Critics noted that paying students to learn could be implemented inexpensively. They worried that this practice could undermine the more expensive initiatives for which reformers had been lobbying for decades. The enthusiasts again had a ready answer: they were pragmatists who only wished to conduct experiments, make observations, and report the results.

Critics even raised philosophical questions. They insisted that paying students to learn interjected commercialization into the schools. They protested that it could not be reconciled with traditional scholastic values. Once again, the enthusiasts had a rejoinder. They claimed that the practice of paying students prepared them to deal with the commercialized practices that permeated their lives.

The critics of monetary incentives acknowledged that commercialism was evident throughout society. They even acknowledged that it was evident in the schools. However, they decried the damage that it caused.

Commercializing Tobacco

When businesspersons were accused of promoting commercial advertising, they did not deny the accusations. They characterized advertising as an essential component of capitalism. They acknowledged that they had applied it to numerous situations and were eager to apply it to many more.

Businesspersons acknowledged that commercial advertising had benefits for them. However, they insisted that it had benefits for other groups, including workers. They noted that workers benefitted because advertising protected their jobs and increased their wages (Frieden, 2006; Whitley, 1999).

Businesspersons pointed proudly to the contribution that advertising had made to America's economy. They highlighted the connection between commercial advertising and innumerable products, including cigarettes (Pennock, 2007; Rabin & Sugarman, 2001).

Early entrepreneurs had asked marketing experts to expand cigarette sales. They wanted the marketers to find ways to make smokers aware of their brands and eager to purchase them.

Aware that only males smoked, the marketers designed cigarette advertisements for men. They attempted to persuade them to purchase the brands that they were advertising. However, then set an additional goal: they would try to persuade males who did not smoke to purchase cigarettes (Hartley, 1990).

When they designed ads for the males, marketers associated cigarettes with brave soldiers, strong workers, and virile athletes. Sometimes they featured famous males with cigarettes; at other times they depicted male cigarette smokers surrounded by fawning females.

The tobacco businesspersons were pleased as the sales of their products increased. They noted that the sales to persons who smoked and to persons who had been nonsmokers rose. They noted that the nonsmokers who tried their products continued to buy them. They were sure that the vast majority of American males would be buying their products.

In spite of their increasing sales, the tobacco businesspersons were remorseful. They realized that sales eventually would reach a plateau. They noted that females, who constituted one half of the consumer population, viewed smoking as an activity that was restricted to males. They concluded that most women would never consider purchasing cigarettes.

When the tobacco businesspersons described their dilemma to marketers, they asked whether female consumers had been permanently alienated. The marketers were optimistic that they could change the attitudes of females. However, they also would have to change the attitudes of males; they would have to persuade them to accept and possibly admire female smokers (Brandt, 2007).

When they designed advertising campaigns to entice females, the marketers depicted women smokers as independent, trendsetting, socially uninhibited, and glamorous. They showcased women smokers who were surrounded by admiring males. They persuaded famous females to endorse smoking. They linked smoking to weight loss.

The marketers introduced cigarette advertisements to females during the first half of the twentieth century. They were gratified as the number of female smokers increased. They noted this number continued to increase in the second half of the century. They also noted that younger females were responding to the ads with special zest (Pennock, 2007).

Tobacco businesspersons were impressed by the marketers' skills in selling cigarettes to females. They asked them to help with other problems. They asked them to transform filter cigarettes, which had been promoted as a product for females, into a product for males (Brandt, 2007). They asked them to transform light beer, which had been promoted as a diet beverage for females, into a drink for males (Lagorce, 2003; Pincas & Loiseau, 2008). In each instance, the marketers succeeded.

Branding

Even though commercial advertising was discernible in every era of American history, it assumed unprecedented dominance during the 1900s. It eventually infused every aspect of American business and culture, including the schools (Cross, 2000).

As they developed greater expertise with commercial advertising, businesspersons were able to use it to expand sales of numerous items. They used it to sell cars, homes, appliances, food, fuel, and the items on which consumers depended. They also used it to sell jewelry, watches, high-fashion clothing, gum, liquor, cigarettes, and many items on which consumers did not depend. They even used it to sell deodorants, mouthwashes, cosmetics, foot powders, and products about which consumers initially were skeptical (Andersen & Strate, 2000).

Marketers and advertisers advised businesspersons that brand visibility was an essential component of commercial advertising. They assured them that it generated approval, respect, admiration, esteem, demand for products, and profits.

As they listened to the assurances about the value of brand visibility, businesspersons inquired why some products had developed extraordinary status. The marketers responded that these products became highly visible because of their reputations for quality, simplicity, reliability, and innovation (Wheeler, 2003).

Marketers detected additional reasons that some products became highly visible. They noted that these products were connected to visual stereotypes. They gave the example of Coca-Cola, which had prospered because of a distinctively shaped bottle. They added that this soft drink also had prospered because of the distinctively styled letters with which its brand name was written (Kitch, 2001).

Marketers were fascinated by cases in which a brand became so visible that it was adopted as the generic name for a product. They identified multiple cases. Persons used the term *Coke* to refer not only to a beverage from the Coca-Cola Company, but to the cola drinks from other companies as well. In a similar manner, they used the term *Kleenex* to refer to multiple brands of tissues.

Marketers wished to create brands that consumers would recognize, admire, and esteem. They devised a process to provide status to little-known brands. They even gave the process a name—branding. By persuading businesspersons to channel 300 billion dollars to branding each year, they transformed the process into a colossal enterprise (Conley, 2008).

COMMERCIALIZING EDUCATION

Businesspersons depended on educators. They depended on them to provide laborers and managers for their firms. They depended on them to help students graduate, enter the workforce, and purchase products. They depended on the educators to personally purchase those products. They depended on the educators to create opportunities for businesspersons to erect buildings, furnish services, and supply equipment.

Businesspersons and educators had cooperated on numerous occasions. For example, they had cooperated on textbooks. Educators admired the formats, illustrations, and pedagogical innovations in professionally produced books. Additionally, most educators recognized that these books were less expensive than materials that they might have created by themselves (Giordano, 2003).

Businesspersons and educators had cooperated on tests. Businesspersons designed tests to assess students' intelligence. In addition to intelligence tests, they devised numerous specialized tests. They developed tests with which teachers and school administrators could measure their students' knowledge of reading, mathematics, science, and most academic subjects. They even prepared standardized tests with which they could measure aptitudes for careers (Giordano, 2005).

Businesspersons and educators cooperated during war. The businesspersons helped by quickly preparing books that were patriotic, relevant to wartime issues, and geared to wartime careers. They even prepared materials to help high school students acquire military skills before they were inducted (Giordano, 2004).

Businesspersons and educators cooperated on technology. The businesspersons created, manufactured, and distributed phonographs, film projectors, radios, and tape recorders. Although they had not created these materials specifically for the schools, they demonstrated how educators could use them to help students learn (Giordano, 2009).

Enthusiasts alleged that businessperson-educator cooperation increased the effectiveness of teachers, the efficiency of school administrators, and the success of students. They added that it also increased national security and economic prosperity. They claimed that this cooperation was evidence that capitalism promoted scholastic excellence. However, they had to confront the skeptics.

Skeptics were not pleased by the collaboration between businesspersons and educators. They noted that the early textbook salespersons had bribed educators. They also noted instances in which educators had demanded payoffs from textbook salespersons. They identified numerous other cases in which either the entrepreneurs or the educators had behaved poorly (Boyles, 2005; Giordano, 2000).

Businesspersons sometimes influenced educators indirectly. For example, they influenced them through the organizational approaches that they showcased. They were particularly fascinated by an early twentieth-century approach that Fredrick Winslow Taylor had championed. They initially referred to this approach as scientific management; they later referred to it as industrial psychology (Gabor, 1999; Kanigel, 1997; Spender & Kijne, 1996).

Taylor commenced a series of experiments to illustrate the conditions under which businesspersons could maximize profits. In these experiments, he altered labor conditions and observed the results. For example, he altered the sizes of factory workers' tools to measure how these changes affected their productivity. He eventually made a list of optimally sized tools for workers in several professions.

Taylor did not stop after he had examined the ways in which tools influenced workers' productivity; he examined numerous other factors. He and his associates looked at the length of labor shifts, duration of rest breaks, frequency of rest breaks, lighting, ventilation, standardization of production, the amounts that workers were paid, the ways in which they were paid, the ways in which feedback was delivered to them, and the frequency with which feedback was delivered.

Taylor assured businesspersons that he could identify the best way to manage workers. However, he warned them that the labor unions would try to prevent them from fully implementing his advice. He emphasized that they had to listen to him and not the union leaders if they truly wished to maximize their profits.

Persons who were excited about Taylor's approach to management wished to implement it in industry. However, they detected additional opportunities to implement it in commerce, transportation, and agriculture. Some of them bragged that it could be implemented in any enterprise where the managers used resources prudently. They proposed to implement it in the schools.

MOTIVATING STUDENTS WITH PUNISHMENTS

Businesspersons wanted laborers to stay on task, work hard, and be productive. Teachers set somewhat similar aspirations for students: they wanted them to behave, study hard, and learn. The teachers exhibited these concerns during the 1800s, which was an era when they relied on punishments to influence their students.

Motivating with Fear

When early teachers encountered children who were not meeting their expectations, they knew what to do: they required them to sit on three-legged stools, face into corners, and wear dunce caps. After they had experimented with these punishments, some of them judged that they were too weak. They searched for more potent punishments.

Teachers began to strike students. Some used their hands; others used branches, yardsticks, or paddles. They hoped that students would change their attitudes and behaviors if they repeatedly were beaten; they hoped that they might change even if they only had seen others beaten.

Like nineteenth-century teachers, some twentieth-century teachers relied on corporal punishment. As late as 2009, they were empowered to use it in over twenty states. The states in which they were allowed to use in included

Alabama, Arizona, Arkansas, Colorado, Florida, Georgia, Idaho, Indiana, Kansas, Kentucky, Louisiana, Mississippi, Missouri, New Mexico, North Carolina, Ohio, Oklahoma, South Carolina, Tennessee, Texas, and Wyoming (Adelson, 2009; "Minorities More Likely," 2008).

Although some modern teachers used corporal punishment, many avoided it. They avoided it because of state bans, school restrictions, parental prohibitions, or personal skepticism about the practice.

Motivating with Compound Punishments

The early teachers punished students regularly. When they punished them, they had the approval of parents, school administrators, school board members, community leaders, and state legislators. In fact, many of them punished students at the behest of these groups

Like their predecessors, modern educators used punishment and intimidation to motivate students. They learned about the effectiveness of these techniques from the early teachers. For example, they learned from them about the effectiveness of low grades.

Teachers hoped that assigning low grades would motivate students; they hoped that students would view the grades as substantive punishments. Nonetheless, many of them wished to increase the impact of low grades. Therefore, they combined low grades with other punishments.

Teachers compounded punishments when they used them simultaneously. Some of them compounded low grades with disapproving scowls. Others compounded them with censorious remarks, angry notes to parents, written comments on report cards, or bans on extracurricular activities.

MOTIVATING WITH MILITARY-STYLE PUNISHMENT

During the 1990s, members of the public were extremely concerned about school safety. As one would expect, they wished to protect students. However, they were also worried about the safety of teachers and school administrators.

Parents, politicians, and members of the public became alarmed when they read and viewed news reports about brazen acts of school violence. They especially were alarmed when youths brought weapons into the schools and then attacked or killed persons (Bonilla, 2000; Egendorf, 2002; Fast, 2008; Hunnicutt, 2006; Newman, 2004).

Critics claimed that the educators inadvertently promoted violence through relaxed disciplinary measures. They recommended that they return to the

severe disciplinary practices of earlier eras. Some adjured them to demonstrate less patience; others demanded that they exhibit no patience. They
used phrases such as "zero tolerance" and "tough love" to characterize the
philosophy that they had in mind (Ayers, Dohrn, & Ayers, 2001; Daniels,
2008; "When 'Tough Love,'" 2007).

Proponents of zero tolerance programs recommended disciplinary
regimens and punishments that were similar to those that the military
employed. In fact, they encouraged the establishment of military-style
regimens.

Some military-style programs, which used disciplinary practices that
were more severe that those that school boards would approve, were managed by private companies. Although they typically were described as
disciplinary boot camps, they occasionally were identified as brat camps
("What's This Thing," 2009). Because they were situated in wilderness
areas, they also were referred to as wilderness programs ("Wilderness
Camp Safety," 2009).

The entrepreneurs who established the military-style training camps had
benefitted from the publicity that accompanied school tragedies. They called
on parents and educators to acknowledge that a military style of training
would prevent future tragedies. However, they lost credibility after they
caused suffering and even the deaths of students ("When 'Tough Love,'"
2007).

The advocates of military-style punishments had to respond to allegations
of neglect and abuse at legal, state, and congressional proceedings. They
insisted that their practices were not any more dangerous than routine physical activities. They protested that they had been criticized unfairly ("Wilderness Camp Safety," 2009). However, they did not appease their critics.

Critics were upset about numerous incidents, including those in which
military-style disciplinarians had neglected or abused children from minority
groups. They asked whether lack of education and training had contributed to
these incidents; they questioned whether racism also had contributed (Reyes,
2006).

Critics raised additional objections about military-style disciplinarians.
They claimed that they had conflicts of interest. They pointed out that these
conflicts were especially egregious because the disciplinarians were accountable to entrepreneurs.

The critics questioned whether the personnel who administered military-
style punishments had been educated about the legal and ethical restrictions
on punishments. They also questioned whether they had been educated about
the physical and psychological consequences of punishments (Manos, 2006;
Szalavitz, 2007; "When 'Tough Love,'" 2007).

MOTIVATING STUDENTS WITH REWARDS

Just as modern-era teachers compounded punishments, they compounded rewards. When teachers enhanced rewards, they sometimes limited the scope of the rewards to their own classrooms. They combined high grades with smiles, complimentary notations on exam papers, commendations before others members of the class, or chances to sit in a prominent classroom location.

Some teachers went beyond their classrooms when they compounded rewards. As examples, they posted exemplary written work on school-wide bulletin boards, announced the names of high-achieving students at school assemblies, or placed the names of the students with high grades in the local newspapers.

Motivating Affluent Students with Money

Teachers and school administrators questioned whether opportunities to earn high grades would motivate students. Some of them questioned whether any exclusively scholastic reward would motivate them. They encouraged parents to supplement grades with tangible rewards; in effect, they advised them to pay children.

When they advised parents to pay children, educators recognized that this practice was controversial. However, they noted that it was hardly novel. Many affluent parents already supplemented good grades with opportunities for their children to travel, engage in hobbies, and play sports.

Some educators and parents wished to create additional opportunities for students; they searched for ways to pay them more money. They were inspired by testimonials about children who had received cash payments and benefitted (Gootman, 2008; Turque, 2008). They noted that the children who received these payments progressed through the grades, graduated from high school, attended college, and became successful community members.

However, the enthusiasts faced a difficulty. Affluent parents already were paying children to learn; poor parents could not afford to pay them.

Motivating Poor Students with Money

The persons who were enthusiastic about paying children to learn worried about impoverished children. They hypothesized that the high rate of school failure among these children was related to the absence of a critical incentive.

They predicted that the poor students would become more successful if they were paid to learn. They convinced philanthropists to supply the money to investigate this prediction.

Although the enthusiasts wished to investigate numerous issues, they used their limited funds to focus on several relatively simple questions. For example, they asked whether bonuses would change the reading habits of impoverished students. To answer this question, they paid students two dollars for each book that they read (Bosman, 2007).

The enthusiasts wished to examine another relatively simple question. They wondered whether bonuses would affect the numbers of times that students were absent from school. To answer this question, they paid students twenty-five dollars if they completed an absence-free period of school attendance (Bosman, 2007).

Although they had been able to assemble a modest amount of money, the enthusiasts needed additional funds for the ambitious studies that they had in mind. They wished to conduct their studies on larger scales and increase the amounts of the cash incentives. After eliciting pledges of nearly eighty million dollars, they were ready to go forward (Gootman, 2008).

The enthusiasts had enough money to make several changes to their studies. As they had pledged, they varied the locations in which they conducted them, involved more participants, and increased the amounts of the bonuses (Gootman, 2008). Although they continued to observe the ways in which payments affected reading, they also observed the ways in which they influenced mathematics, English, and science.

The enthusiasts made additional changes to their studies. They expanded the types of circumstances under which students would receive bonuses. In New York City, they gave students bonuses for passing tests as well as graduating from high school (Davis, 2007). They even began to give bonuses to a completely new group—teachers.

Not all educators and parents supported the student bonuses (Deere, 2002; Guernsey, 2009; Turque, 2008). They feared that the bonuses would engender commercialism, which they viewed as a destructive force in children's lives (Fox, 1996; Jenkins, 2006; McCall, 2007; Quart, 2003).

The bonus enthusiasts were not silenced by their critics. They retorted that the cash bonuses were worthwhile because they helped persons immediately and then again later in their lives. They explained that they enabled them to excel immediately as students and later as workers, consumers, and taxpayers.

Critics had additional reasons for objecting to the bonus programs. They pointed out that the goals of education included emotional maturity, self-confidence, wisdom, ethical behavior, and citizenship. They predicted that paying students to learn would undermine these goals.

Critics were especially censorious of the bonus programs that paid teachers. They predicted that some teachers would be unwilling to instruct students who could not make the gains that instructors needed to qualify for bonuses. They worried that other teachers would exploit students in order to qualify for bonuses (Deere, 2002).

Critics even had political reasons for opposing bonuses. They contrasted the modest sum that was needed to implement bonus programs with the much larger sum that was needed to hire qualified teachers, rebuild obsolete educational facilities, expand technology, replace antiquated textbooks, and purchase new school equipment. They worried that some politicians would support bonus programs simply because they were a relatively cheap way to address endemic educational problems.

EXAMINING ADVICE FROM BUSINESSPERSONS

Early teachers motivated students with punishments; they tried grimaces, scowls, low grades, graduation delays, spanking, and paddling. Additionally, they tried rewards.

Later teachers paid attention to the practices of the early educators. However, they also paid attention to advice from businesspersons. The businesspersons gave suggestions about textbooks, testing, school design, and technology; they even gave them suggestions about motivating students.

Activity 3.1

You might wish to examine motivational practices. You could look at both punishments and rewards. You could rely on Table 3.1.

Table 3.1 identifies eight scholastic practices: teacher gestures, corporal punishment, grading, academic penalties, military-style punishment, monetary incentives paid to students by their parents, monetary incentives paid to students through the schools, and monetary incentives paid to teachers through the schools.

To complete this table, indicate an advantage and a disadvantage for each practice. Finally, provide explanations for your observations. You could complete the table by yourself, with another reader, or with a small group of readers. You could rely on the information in this chapter, the books that are cited in it, additional books, or your personal experiences.

Table 3.1. Rewards and Punishments

Practice	Advantage	Disadvantage	Explanation
Teacher Gesture			
Corporal Punishment			
Grading			
Academic Penalty			
Military-Style Punishment			
Parents Pay Students			
Schools Pay Students			
Schools Pay Teachers			

Activity 3.2

You could examine motivational practices from a distinct perspective. You could consider the ways in which groups reacted to them. You could rely on Table 3.2.

Table 3.2 lists four motivational practices: academic penalties, military-style discipline, monetary incentives that were paid to students by parents, and monetary incentives that were paid to students by the schools. It provides opportunities to indicate the ways in which teachers, principals, members of school boards, and local businesspersons reacted to these practices.

Use symbols to complete this table. Use the symbol – to indicate that the members of a group gave a low degree of support to practices. Use the symbol –/+ for moderate support and the symbol + for high support. Explain the basis for the symbols that you selected.

Table 3.2.   Reactions to Motivational Techniques

Group	Motivational Practice*				Rationale
	Academic Penalties	Military-Style Discipline	Parents Pay Students	Schools Pay Students	
Parents					
Teachers					
Principals					
School Board Members					
Business-persons					

* (–) Low Support
(–/+) Moderate Support
(+) High Support

Activity 3.3

You might wish to examine practices that promoted commercialism in society and the schools. You could rely on Table 3.3.

Table 3.3 gives you the chance to compare paying students to learn with a commercial practice—marketing cigarettes. It also gives you the chances to compare paying students with several scholastic practices on which educators and businesspersons collaborated. It lists four practices: wartime education, technology-based education, textbooks, and standardized tests.

To complete this table, note similarities and differences between paying students to learn and other practices. Finally, explain your observations.

Table 3.3.   Commercializing Non-Scholastic and Scholastic Practices

Practice	Paying Students		Explanation
	Similarity	*Difference*	
Cigarettes			
Wartime Education Programs			
School Technology			
Textbooks			
Standardized Tests			

Activity 3.4

You could select another way to examine the practices on which business-persons and educators collaborated. You could examine the public's attitudes toward those practices. You could use Table 3.4

Table 3.4 identifies six collaborative practices: publishing textbooks, developing standardized tests, designing school buildings, disseminating technology, implementing wartime school programs, and paying poor students to learn.

This table also identifies three eras: the period before World War II, the period after World War II, and the current period. With the exception of paying poor students to learn, the listed practices were evident during all three eras.

Use symbols to complete this table. Use the symbol – to indicate that the public gave a low degree of support to a practice. Use the symbol –/+ for moderate support and the symbol + for high support. Finally, explain the basis for the symbols that you selected.

Table 3.4. Shifting Attitudes Toward Businessperson-Educator Cooperation

	*Public's Attitudes**			
Practice	*Before World War II*	*After World War II*	*Current*	*Explanation*
Textbooks				
Standardized Tests				
School Buildings				
Technology				
Wartime School Programs				
Monetary Incentives to Poor Students	*n/a*	*n/a*		

* (–) Low Support
(–/+) Moderate Support
(+) High Support

SUMMARY

Some persons transferred business practices into the schools. For example, they rewarded students with cash bonuses. However, critics censured them for neutralizing traditional scholastic practices, promoting materialism, and undermining more substantive scholastic reforms.

Chapter 4

Do Researchers See That Which They Choose to See?

Scientists may be no different from lay people when it comes to a message that strikes a chord in them.

—Gina Kolata, 1998

Critics claimed that researchers were influenced by preconceptions, intuitions, and conflicts of interest. They substantiated their allegations with examples from numerous fields, including education.

BEHAVIORAL SCIENTISTS

Researchers had little difficulty persuading some persons to accept their explanations about education. They won the support of groups that already agreed with them. Although they were embraced by the persons whose opinions they validated, they were shunned by those whose opinions they challenged.

Critics worried that researchers had succumbed to preconceptions, intuitions, and conflicts of interest. They found examples on which to base their concerns.

Psychologists

During the 1920s and the 1930s, industrial psychologists conducted experiments at a Chicago factory. They were attempting to determine the ways in which changes affected workers.

41

The psychologists kept records of the original conditions and the modifications that they made. The laborers originally had been paid according to the number of items that they produced. Although they continued to be paid for their productivity, they were subjected to new formulas.

The psychologists made numerous modifications. They altered the number of rest breaks that workers could take, the lengths of the breaks, and the spans of their workdays. They even altered the lighting and the air quality in the area where they labored. As they made these alternations, they observed the workers' reactions.

The psychologists were confused because the workers improved their job performance in response to every type of alteration. Although workers became more productive in response to workplace changes, they raised their productivity to even higher levels after those changes were eliminated.

Decades after the original experiments were conducted, psychologists examined the records from the Chicago factory. They noted that the managers at the factory had not hid their experiment from the workers. In fact, the managers called attention to the experiments by sequestering workers, dismissing two of them for inappropriate behavior, and even discussing the experiments with them. They hypothesized that the workers' awareness of the experiments had affected their behaviors.

Psychologists eventually adopted a theory to explain the events at the Chicago factory. They theorized that the workers' awareness of the experiment and its goals had compromised the research. Because the Chicago factory was named the Hawthorne Works, they referred to the subjects in the experiment as victims of the *Hawthorne effect.*

The laborers at the Hawthorne Works might have increased their productivity because of their awareness of the experiment. However, they could have been influenced by other factors. For example, they could have increased their productivity to avoid being laid off during a period of high employment (Leonard, 2009). They also may have been influenced by factors such as workplace camaraderie and an unusually collegial relationship with their supervisor.

The theorists who devised the Hawthorne effect suspected that the researchers at the Chicago plant had compromised their investigation. However, some critics were equally suspicious of theorists. They complained that their eagerness to find an explanation had compromised their own deliberations. They judged that this eagerness may have prevented them from detecting the original situation's complexity. They worried that it later prevented them from abandoning their theory, even after it was clear that it was flawed (Kolata, 1998).

Anthropologists

Psychologists and businesspersons devised the Hawthorne effect to explain the unexpected results of experimental studies. Because the explanation struck them as useful, they espoused it for decades. They espoused it even after they knew that they had made questionable assumptions.

The proponents of the Hawthorne effect had discerned weaknesses in the experimental studies at a Chicago factory. Disenchanted with experimental research, some of their colleagues were eager to devise a new way to gather information. They hoped that scholars in other fields would help them design a type of research to complement their distinctive views about human behavior. They were attracted to pioneering cultural anthropologists, such as Margaret Mead.

Margaret Mead was a student at Columbia University during the 1920s. Wishing to examine residents in a remote non-Western society, she journeyed to Samoa. She attempted to unobtrusively observe the native inhabitants, their environment, and their culture.

Although Mead may have been unobtrusive when she was in Samoa, she attracted a great deal of attention after she left. She published a book in which she contended that the Samoan youths resided in a society without pejorative attitudes towards sex. As a result, the Samoans could experiment freely with sex and not suffer the emotional problems that were typical in Western cultures.

Some readers praised Mead for her originality, insight, and wisdom; others lambasted her for censuring their culture, values, and traditions. Although many persons disagreed with Mead's interpretation of her observations, they did not challenge the observations themselves. Derek Freeman changed that situation in the early 1980s.

Like Mead, Freeman was a cultural anthropologist who visited Samoa, participated in the island society, and observed the residents. However, he did not draw the same conclusions as Mead. In fact, he dismissed Mead's depiction of Samoan society as an anthropological myth (Freeman, 1983, 1999).

Although he was sure that Mead made mistakes, Freeman had to confront her supporters. The supporters demanded that he explain how Mead could have erred. Freeman replied that Mead erred because she went to Samoa with firm expectations and then made observations to confirm those expectations. He even had an explanation for the answers that the Samoans gave to Mead's questions: he conjectured that they gave her the answers that would please her.

Some critics sided with Freeman; others sided with Mead. Each group attracted persons who shared their attitudes and alienated those who did not share them. Although the disputants argued for decades, they changed few minds (Foerstel & Gilliam, 1992; Holmes, 1987; Orans, 1996). One observer conjectured that Mead, Freeman, and their respective allies all exhibited the same fault—an inability to rise above their preconceptions (Levy, 1984).

EDUCATIONAL SCIENTISTS

Critics detected biases among the behavioral scientists who tried to explain human actions. They found examples to underscore their accusations. They made similar accusations about educators.

Physical Therapists

During the 1950s, a five-member research team was attempting to devise ways to help persons with brain injuries. Glenn Doman, a physical therapist, and Carl Delacato, an educational psychologist, were members of that team. They and their colleagues hypothesized that each stage of physical development contributed in a special way to neurological development. They predicted that brain-injured patients who reenacted movements from these stages would regain lost neurological functions.

Doman and Delacato developed relatively simple clinical activities. For example, they encouraged brain-injured persons to crawl like young children. After experimenting with these activities, they observed remarkable results. Although they attracted some attention with their initial claims, they attracted much greater attention when they claimed that their distinctive clinical activities had helped children with speech and learning problems (Delacato, 1963).

Doman and Delacato believed that early gross motor movements were critical to subsequent learning. They claimed that the reenactment of these movements restored underdeveloped or lost learning aptitudes. Although some professional colleagues supported them, others disagreed (Bratt, 1989; Cummins, 1988; Freeman, 1967; Thomas & LeWinn, 1969). The disputants even disagreed about the terms that they should use when referring to the Doman-Delacato techniques; they interchanged terms such as *creeping-crawling, patterning,* and *sensorimotor patterning techniques* (Bratt, 1989; Cohen, Birch, & Taft, 1970; Jurcisin, 1968).

The Doman-Delacato activities were distinctive because of their format: they did not resemble the prevalent treatments for persons with brain injuries. They were distinctive because of the locations in which they were offered: they were available only at private clinics. However, they had another feature that set them apart—the aggressive manner in which they were marketed.

Doman marketed his activities in a popular book about children with brain injuries (Doman, 2005). He also marketed them in the materials that he wrote about children with non-neurological learning problems. He even marketed them in books about children who were developing normally and learning effectively.

In the books that he published from the 1960s through the 1980s, Doman advised parents that his techniques would help learners with problems that resulted from disabilities or giftedness. He repeatedly made the point that his techniques had been validated by research (Doman & Doman, 2002, 2005, 2006; Doman, Doman, & Aisen, 1984).

Doman and Delacato benefited by associating themselves indirectly with a reputable medical organization. After all, they had published their initial report in a journal of the American Medical Association (Doman, Spitz, Zucman, Delacato, & Doman, 1960). However, most medical researchers eventually concluded that the Doman-Delacato activities were ineffective (American Academy of Pediatrics, 1982). Undeterred by this criticism, Doman, Delacato, and their enthusiasts published books, marketed learning kits, operated clinics, and attracted clients.

Professors

The early teachers were not given teaching supplies or textbooks. Although they had limited resources, they had substantial responsibilities. They designed curricula, improvised learning materials, and taught students. Because their schools typically comprised a single room, they grouped kindergarteners, older students, and adolescents together.

As towns and cities became more populous, community leaders hired specialists to teach in kindergartens, elementary schools, and high schools. They also hired school psychologists, remedial reading specialists, speech-language pathologists, occupational therapists, special educators, physical educators, vocational educators, school nurses, clerks, cooks, and grounds-keepers. They appointed principals, superintendents, and boards to manage the schools.

Members of the public detected the staffing changes that the school administrators were making. They also detected other changes. They watched as they built multi-classroom buildings, arranged school transportation, purchased textbooks, implemented district-wide curricula, and administered standardized tests.

Although many persons approved of the changes, others worried that schools were becoming too bloated, complex, and bureaucratic. They feared that the teachers in them were unable to meet the needs of individual students.

Birth of Progressive Education

Critics decried many of the changes that were taking place in the schools. They reminisced nostalgically about the early teachers, who had greater responsibilities and authority. Although they wished to return to the practices of earlier eras, they paradoxically referred to themselves as progressive educators (Giordano, 2000).

The progressive educators even had a current example to illustrate their goal: they wanted American teachers to copy Great Britain's early childhood educators. The British educators had reduced regimentation through individualized schedules, curricula, learning materials, and instructional activities. They had integrated academic learning with physical activities, artistic experiences, vocational development, and play (Hertzberg & Stone, 1971; Hutt, 1989; Rathbone, 1971; Rounds, 1975; Taylor, 1971; Whitbread, 1972).

The professors who endorsed progressive education made personal adjurations to the teacher candidates in the normal schools, colleges, and universities. However, they took additional steps to spread their philosophy; they organized a professional society, published journals, wrote textbooks, and conducted research studies.

The professors who espoused progressive programs were enthusiastic, articulate, and prolific. They gave explicit advice to school administrators. For example, they advised them to hire master teachers for their programs. The school administrators, who were having difficulty persuading high school graduates to become instructors, hardly could hire master teachers. They concluded that this suggestion and many others were impractical (Giordano, 2000, 2009).

Death of Progressive Education

The professors who endorsed progressive education had a hard time spreading their philosophy for practical reasons. They also had difficulty for political reasons. Some of them were social activists who viewed communism as the solution for the severe economic problems of the 1930s.

Conservative ideologues placed political and social pressure on the progressive educators during the Great Depression. Nonetheless, they could not prevent them from attracting recruits. When they increased that pressure during World War II, they had greater success. They claimed that the progressive educators, whom they depicted as communists or the dupes of the communists, threatened national security. They substantiated their accusations with politically inflammatory passages that progressive educators had written.

Conservatives claimed that the progressive educators were dangerous because they used their positions in universities to influence future teachers. However, they even found disquieting passages in the textbooks that they had written for elementary and high school students. They argued that the progressive educators were using the textbooks to erode children's respect for government.

After they were battered in the newspapers and magazines, the progressive educators had difficulty recruiting new members, retaining current members, attracting readers for their journal, and gathering the funds to run their organization. They eventually had to dissolve their association (Giordano, 2000, 2009).

Reincarnation of Progressive Education

After the demise of the progressive education movement, some American teachers and school administrators were still passionate about its philosophy and practices. They looked for an opportunity to reestablish them. During the 1960s, they believed that the open-classroom movement was the opportunity for which they had been searching.

The proponents of open classrooms had distinctive views about kindergartens. They believed that kindergartens should be egalitarian communities in which the youngsters made decisions about learning materials, assessments, schedules, curricula, and instructional practices.

The enthusiasts recommended that all elementary school teachers employ practices similar to those that they had recommended for kindergarten teachers. For example, they recommended that they empower students to decide when to leave one learning group and move to another.

Although enthusiasts were ready to allow children to roam freely about the schools, they were worried that doors, walls, and hallways would restrict them. To solve this problem, they removed walls from educational facilities that already had been erected. To reduce problems in new buildings, they made sure that they were designed in the open manner of gymnasiums (Blitz, 1973; Silberman, 1973; Thibadeau, 1976).

Enthusiasts of open schools encouraged learners to move freely among teachers and clusters of learners. As for teachers, they advised them to abandon traditional practices and rely instead on informal instructional techniques (Howes, 1974; Morgan, Richman, & Taylor, 1981; Rathbone,

1971; Taylor, 1972). They gave them advice that was tailored for instruction in reading, writing, literature, mathematics, and social studies (Berger & Winters, 1973; Hoffman, 1978; Kohl, 1974).

The enthusiasts had advice about learning materials. After warning that textbooks and workbooks promoted scholastic regimentation, they encouraged teachers to replace them with materials that were more practical, interactive, stimulating, and entertaining (Ascheim, 1973; Kohl, 1969; Sabaroff & Hanna, 1974; Smith, 1974; Thomas, 1975).

The enthusiasts, who were wary of regimented learning materials, also were wary of regimented assessments. They adjured teachers to discard standardized tests and personally observe the peculiar ways in which each student reacted to individualized learning materials (Giordano, 2005). They urged them to use these informal observations to help students. They also encouraged them to share their observations with parents, who wished to be reassured about the value of open classrooms.

Second Death of Progressive Education

The critics, who recognized that enthusiasts were opinionated about open classrooms, were equally opinionated. They worried that teachers who lacked the temperaments for open classrooms would spend a good deal of time shielding children from the many distractions within unconventionally designed schools.

In addition to raising questions about teachers' dispositions, critics raised questions about their skills. They suggested that only master teachers had the skills to abandon educational approaches that were designed by experts, supported by textbooks, and validated by standardized tests. They identified instances in which teachers without these skills had failed in open classrooms.

Critics even questioned the research studies on which the open classrooms were based. They noted that these studies relied on informal observations by enthusiasts. They worried that the enthusiasts, whom they characterized as romantics, were blinded by biases and conflicts of interest.

EXAMINING HISTORICAL AND CURRENT ADVICE

Critics distrusted researchers who were influenced by preconceptions, intuitions, and conflicts of interest. They found examples among psychologists, anthropologists, physical therapists, and educators.

Some psychologists had been investigating reports about employees' unpredictable behaviors. They concluded that the employees were victims of the Hawthorne effect. After they learned that the original reports could have been erroneous, they still retained their conclusions.

Anthropologists used observations about South Pacific islanders to explain adolescent behaviors. After they were advised of irregularities in those observations, they kept their explanation.

In another case, physical therapists claimed that bodily exercises helped persons with brain injuries, learning problems, and speech problems. They claimed that they also helped children who were developing normally. Although they were informed that their claims could not be confirmed, they stood by them.

Educators made observations about the benefits of communal learning. They advised their colleagues to adapt schoolhouse architecture, pedagogical practices, learning materials, and assessment procedures. After they realized that their observations could not be confirmed, they still provided the same advice.

Activity 4.1

You might wish to examine researchers. You could consider the influence of biases on them. You could use Table 4.1.

Table 4.1 lists four historical incidents. It identifies the incidents that were associated with the Hawthorne effect, *Coming of Age in Samoa,* the Doman-Delacato approach, and the open classroom. It gives you chances to assess whether the scholars that were involved with these initiatives were influenced by conflicts of interest, preconceptions, and intuitions.

Use numerals to complete this table. Use the numeral *1* to indicate that a factor had a low level of impact on the scholars. Use the numeral *2* for medium impact and the numeral *3* for high impact. Finally, explain why you assigned the numerals that you selected. You can rely on the information in this chapter, the books that are cited in it, additional books, and your personal experiences.

Activity 4.2

You could examine research incidents from another perspective. You might decide to consider the ways in which members of the public reacted to them. You could rely on Table 4.2.

Table 4.1.   Scholars React to Research

| | Reaction* | | | |
Incident	Conflict	Preconception	Intuition	Explanation
Hawthorne Effect				
Coming of Age in Samoa				
Doman-Delacato Approach				
Open Classroom				

*(1) Low Impact
(2) Medium Impact
(3) High Impact

Table 4.2 list two historical incidents: the Doman-Delacato approach and the open-classroom movement. It gives you opportunities to indicate whether members of the public were influenced by preconceptions and intuitions when they reacted to these incidents.

You can use numeral to complete this table. Use the numerals in the legend. Finally, explain the basis for the numerals that you selected.

Activity 4.3

You might wish to examine the ways in which the public reacted to historical and recent research incidents. You could rely on Table 4.3.

Table 4.3 identifies a historical research incident: the open-classroom movement. It allows you to identify a recent incident. You can identify the second incident by yourself, with another reader, or with a small group of readers.

To complete this table, hypothesize about the degrees to which members of public relied on preconceptions and intuitions. You can use numerals to express their reactions to each incident. Use the numerals in the legend. Finally, explain your selections.

Table 4.2. Public Reactions to Research

Incident	Reaction*		Explanation
	Preconception	Intuition	
Doman-Delacato Approach			
Open Classroom			

*(1) Low Impact
(2) Medium Impact
(3) High Impact

Table 4.3. Public Reactions to Past and Recent Research

Incident	Reaction*		Explanation
	Preconception	Intuition	
Open Classroom			
Other:			

*(1) Low Impact
(2) Medium Impact
(3) High Impact

SUMMARY

As researchers investigated problems, they were influenced by preconceptions, intuitions, and conflicts of interest. When members of the public reacted to their investigations, they were influenced by the same factors.

Chapter 5

Are School Uniforms Similar to Motorcycle Helmets?

Our public schools should be able to require their students to wear school uniforms.

—President Bill Clinton
[as quoted by Mitchell, 1996]

When economists and engineers conducted investigations, they had to make decisions about the types of data they would collect and the amounts they would share. Educational researchers also had to make these decisions.

ECONOMISTS AND COOKS

Economists used a metaphor to castigate their rivals: they accused them of "cooking" data (Baker, 2006). They assumed that disreputable analysts would know precisely what they meant.

Most persons associated cooking with savory dishes, holiday scents, enticing restaurants, open-air markets, and other positive experiences. Nonetheless, they conceded that cooks had a peculiar trait: they could be extremely selective.

When cooks trimmed meat, poultry, fish, vegetables, or fruits, they left only select portions. When they applied gravies, sauces, and spices, they enhanced select aspects of foods. When they designated the order in which they would serve the courses of meals, they highlighted select dishes. When they made rooms, tables, or place settings into culinary stimulants, they relied on select environmental features.

Economists understood that all professionals were selective. Nonetheless, they wished to single out those professionals who excessively trimmed,
enhanced, or suppressed data. Researchers in other fields, who were fascinated by this rhetoric, began to accuse their own colleagues of cooking data.

VEHICULAR SAFETY ENGINEERS

Industrial psychologists ruminated about the early twentieth-century experiments at the Hawthorne Works. They read about workers who demonstrated
odd behaviors. Many of them first learned about the experiments from
college textbooks. Confused by the ways in which the laborers acted, they
looked for an explanatory theory. They were attracted to one that linked the
workers' odd behaviors to their awareness of the experiment.

The psychologists initially did not realize that the textbooks on which they
had relied were inaccurate (Olson, Verley, Santos, & Salas, 2004). When
they later discovered that the authors of those books had oversimplified their
descriptions of the events, they continued to espouse the theory that was
based on those descriptions.

The psychologists may have been so eager to solve problems that they
sacrificed their scientific objectivity. Researchers in other fields may have
demonstrated the same sort of impatience.

Automobile Researchers

Safety experts were eager to determine the reasons for traffic deaths. When
they commenced their investigations, they examined somewhat obvious
factors. As examples, they examined the ways in which weather, alcohol,
drugs, trucking, road design, maintenance, congestion, and seat belts affected
automobile accidents (McMillan & Lapham, 2006; "More Than Half of All
Traffic Deaths," 2004).

Investigators eventually examined factors that were somewhat difficult to
discern. For example, they examined whether lack of sleep was related to traffic
deaths (Nagourney, 2008). They also looked at aggressive driving, cell phone
use, and roadside distractions ("Cell Phone Driving Laws," 2009; Lassetter,
2009). They looked at emotions such as road rage (Galovski, Malta, &
Blanchard, 2006; Garase, 2006). They even asked whether the duress that drivers experienced in heavy traffic triggered fatal heart attacks (Ensha, 2009).

After asking about obvious and less obvious causes of traffic deaths,
researchers turned their attention to the factors from still another category.
They asked whether some of the devices that were created to prevent traffic

deaths inadvertently promoted them (Evans, 2007; Mayor, 2007). Radar, which had been implemented to deter speeding, had created a market for devices with which drivers could evade it; it inadvertently may have increased recklessness driving.

Car horns, like automotive radar, had been designed as safety devices. Nonetheless, some persons used them to bully motorists. Researchers asked whether aggressive drivers behaved even more recklessly because of the ways in which they employed horns ("New York City Drivers," 2009). They asked whether other safety devices, such as pedestrian walkways, traffic signals, detours, roadside rest stops, billboards, and lane closures, sometimes promoted reckless driving.

Motorcycle Researchers

When researchers decided to study the causes of motorcycle fatalities, they could have extrapolated information from automobile safety engineers. They could have examined information about road conditions, traffic patterns, weather, and factors that seemed to be obvious contributors to accidents. They could have examined information about drivers' attitudes, emotions, habits, and those factors that might have more subtle connections to road fatalities. They could have examined information about devices that had been implemented to create safety but that also could create peril.

The motorcycle researchers decided to commence original investigations to explain the increasing numbers of persons who were dying on motorcycles. They focused on fatalities at the end of the twentieth century and the beginning of the twenty-first century (Stella, Cooke, & Sprivulis, 2002; Ullrich, 2003).

Like the automobile engineers, the motorcycle researchers began by look-ing for obvious factors. They noted that manufacturers recently had begun to produce machines that accelerated quicker and traveled faster than earlier models. They questioned whether more powerful machines were responsible for more fatalities (Sepkowitz, 2008).

Although the motorcycle researchers looked for the obvious causes of road deaths, they also looked at some less obvious factors. They noted that persons who once eschewed motorcycles began to use them because the bikes con-sumed less gas. They wondered whether the changing characteristics of cyclists explained the increasing fatalities ("High Gas Prices Cause Surge," 2008).

Motorcycle researchers identified another change in the characteristics of cyclists: more seniors were riding them. They reasoned that older riders, who could afford extremely powerful machines, were driving with abandon as they tried to recapture the spirit of youth ("Motorcycle Deaths Among Boomers," 2005).

After noting that the probability of death in motorcycle accidents was much higher than that in car accidents, motorcycle researchers conjectured that equipment might be a cause of fatalities. They examined two types of safety equipment. They looked at vehicular components: signal lights, mirrors, tires, headlights, collision bars, reflectors, and braking systems. They even examined motorcycle airbags (Wald, 2007a). They also looked at driver-worn accessories: clothing to reduce injuries to chests, backs, shoulders, knees, legs, elbows, hands, feet, eyes, and faces.

The researchers focused an extraordinary amount of attention on a particular driver-worn accessory—the motorcycle helmet. They pointed out that many motorcycle riders had decided that they would not wear helmets. They were convinced that this decision was the chief reason that so many of them were dying.

The advocates for helmets pointed out that the changes in federal and state regulations had enabled the cyclists to abandon helmets. They urged lawmakers to once again mandate helmets for all cyclists (Mertz & Weiss, 2008; "Motorcycle Deaths Among Boomers," 2005; National Center for Statistics and Analysis, 1998; Poole, 2005; Wald, 2007b; Yaukey & Benincasa, 2008).

In spite of intense lobbying, the advocates for helmets had limited success. By 2009, only nineteen states and the District of Columbia required all cyclists to wear helmets. Three states refused to set any helmet requirements. The majority of the states established helmet requirements solely for younger riders (Jones, 2009).

GANG SPECIALISTS

When they began to study road fatalities, the motorcycle researchers could have extrapolated procedures and information from the automobile researchers. They could have examined the impact of obvious, subtle, and counterintuitive factors. Instead, they decided to concentrate on the helmet.

Researchers who studied numerous types of problems had to make choices about the scope of their studies. In fields such as sociology, criminology, and psychology, they were concerned about the high numbers of urban youths who joined gangs. They hoped to determine the reasons that they were attracted to gangs; they hoped to reduce that attraction.

Pragmatic Specialists

During the late nineteenth century, Jane Addams wished to lure immigrant children from Chicago's street gangs. She conceived an original plan. Instead of basing that plan on a precisely defined theory, she developed a highly pragmatic scheme. She enticed youths to an alternative school at which they would have chances to read, study academics, speak in English, prepare for careers, play sports, participate in the arts, engage in hobbies, socialize, and play (Giordano, 2009).

In addition to reaching out to adolescents, Addams invited young children into her school. She provided them with an indoor nursery and an outdoor playground. She gave them nourishing food, clean clothing, and even areas where they could bathe. She gave them medicine, inoculations, dental care, and health care.

Addams also offered helpful services to parents. She provided women who had been abused with an emergency shelter and counselors. She surrounded women and men with lawyers, job recruiters, union organizers, and numerous other professionals.

Addams was an early specialist who was concerned about the disproportionate numbers of minority youths in gangs. Throughout the twentieth century, other specialists shared her concerns. However, many of them approached the problem differently. They stopped focusing on programs to help youths and concentrated on theories to explain their behaviors.

Ideological Specialists

Some gang specialists were ideologues. They argued that the numbers of minority participants in gangs had been grossly misrepresented. They added that persons with racial and ethnic prejudices were responsible for the misrepresentation.

Other specialists admitted that gangs had an unusual impact on minority youths. They were alarmed about the great impact of the gangs on African Americans and Hispanic Americans. As they looked for an explanation, some of them conjectured that minority youths joined gangs to compensate for the status and resources that had been denied to them in mainstream society.

Although some specialists depicted minority youths as victims, others depicted them as predators. They argued that they joined gangs because they were socially, and possibly even genetically, predisposed to violence and confrontation (Gabbidon, 2007; Russell-Brown, 2006; Webster, 2007).

Specialists came up with many more reasons to explain why minority youths joined gangs. They suggested that they might join because they were unfairly stereotyped in the news, misrepresented in the popular media, oppressed by an empowered social class, or victimized by economic, medical, and educational problems.

Gang Garb

Although educators were confused about the reasons that gangs flourished, some of them believed that they could reduce their influence. They found cases in which gang members wore clothing that incorporated the names or logos of professional sports teams, clothing manufacturers, restaurants, and universities. Once they had identified gang garb, they proposed to ban it.

School administrators had several reasons for believing that bans on gang clothing would be effective. They hoped that the bans would prevent gangs from recognizing the members of other gangs, recruiting new members, and attacking innocent students who inadvertently wore the symbols of rival gangs.

School administrators advised students about clothing bans and the punishments for violating them. They assured parents and community members that the bans would reduce the influence of the gangs in schools. They appealed for community support (Capozzoli & McVey, 2000; Goldstein & Kodluboy, 1998; Howell & Lynch, 2000; Lal, Lal, & Achilles, 1993).

Critics challenged the school administrators who banned gang clothing. They scolded them for taking actions that went beyond their authority. When they were unable to persuade the school administrators to back down, they went to court. They were pleased when the courts agreed with them (Burke, 1994).

After school administrators lost court challenges, they asked their state legislators to help them; they asked them to pass laws authorizing them to ban gang-associated clothing. By 2009, legislators had enacted laws of this sort in California, Iowa, Missouri, Nevada, New Jersey, Tennessee, Texas, Utah, Virginia, and Washington (Institute for Intergovernmental Research, 2009).

SCHOOL REFORMERS

At the beginning of the 1900s, American citizens were unsure about how to deal with many problems in the schools. A century later, they still were unsure. They had to solve problems that affected students, teachers, and school administrators; they also had to solve problems that involved school buildings, textbooks, technology, curricula, tests, instructional strategies, and school policies (Giordano, 2009).

Although some school problems were confined to the schools, others originated in children's homes and neighborhoods. The teachers believed that all of these problems were connected. For example, they had a difficult time solving scholastic problems when students were malnourished, impoverished, unhealthy, unable to communicate in English, threatened by violence, oppressed by gangs, or addicted to drugs (Giordano, 2009).

Ideological Reformers

When they attempted to solve scholastic and community problems, school reformers frequently championed doctrinaire solutions. For example, politically conservative ideologues were sure that many problems originated with declining patriotism in the schools. They were confident that patriotic textbooks and patriotic academic programs would eliminate these problems. They became furious when liberals disagreed (Giordano, 2003, 2009).

The liberals denigrated the patriotic materials and practices that the conservatives championed. In fact, liberals claimed that these materials and practices had caused some of the problems that they were supposed to reduce. They insisted that the patriotic materials be removed from the schools.

Pragmatic Reformers

Although some school reformers were ideologues, others were pragmatists. The pragmatists, who searched for expedient solutions, demonstrated their resourcefulness on numerous occasions.

The pragmatists advised school administrators to rely on technology. They encouraged them to adopt technology because it would stimulate students, help them learn, and prepare them for critical careers. They added that it also would reduce the cost of instruction. They concluded that it had impressive benefits for educators, employers, students, and those entrepreneurs who manufactured technological devices.

The pragmatists demonstrated their resourcefulness again when they advised school administrators to use flexible student schedules. They pointed out that these schedules allowed adolescents to maintain part-time jobs. They added that they were especially valuable during wars because students could stay in school and make critical contributions to national defense (Giordano, 2004, 2009).

Feuds

During the second half of the twentieth century, school reformers turned their attention to multiple problems: literacy instruction, textbook bias, racial segregation, school dropouts, bilingual instruction, teacher unionization, special education, school violence, substance abuse, and standardized testing (Giordano, 2009).

School reform groups, which comprised conservative ideologues, liberal ideologues, and pragmatists, had difficulty agreeing about the problems that they should tackle. When they did agree on a problem, they still argued about whether they should look for a simple or comprehensive solution.

Unable to agree about problems and solutions, the reformers inevitably disagreed about budgets. They disagreed about the amount of money that they should allocate in order to make scholastic changes; they disagreed heatedly about the amount of money that they should allocate to assessment.

Enthusiasts depicted standardized testing as a relatively inexpensive solution to complex and severe problems; they urged school administrators to use it extensively. Opponents disagreed about the benefits of standardized testing; they urged school administrators to eschew it. The feuding between the enthusiasts and opponents of testing confused most parents, community members, and politicians; it also confused many educators (Giordano, 2005).

School reformers continued to search for solutions to complex educational problems. Wishing to attract parents, community members, and politicians, they searched for a simple-to-explain and cheap-to-implement solution. During the 1990s, they believed that they had found this type of solution—school uniforms.

School Uniforms

School reformers recommended that students wear uniforms. They were aware this idea was not novel; they conceded that students in military, religious, and private schools had sported uniforms for centuries (Bryk, Lee, & Holland, 1993). Although they admitted that uniforms were not new, they argued that they had numerous benefits.

Enthusiast claimed that school uniforms had self-evident benefits. They noted that they imposed standardization onto school environments, reduced the pressure to purchase expensive clothing, and lessened the chances that gang-associated clothing would provoke violence. They added that the uniforms had still more positive features.

Proponents claimed that students who wore uniforms exhibited relatively few behavioral, emotional, and social problems (Grapes, 2000; Kohn, 1998; Loesch, 1995). They claimed that they attended school regularly and achieved high levels in their academic studies. To strengthen their claims, they noted that the United States Department of Education had endorsed uniforms (Mitchell, 1996).

Some parents, community leaders, and politicians were excited. They hoped that uniforms could solve some of the truly wrenching problems in the schools. They hoped that they would affect students who were dropping out, becoming pregnant, abusing drugs, and joining gangs. They hoped that they would affect students who were carrying guns and attacking their peers at school (Fast, 2008; Newman, 2004). Although they had high hopes, they had to silence skeptics.

The skeptics questioned whether school administrators had violated students' rights when they crafted school uniform policies (Hudson, 2004). However, they also questioned the benefits of those policies.

The skeptics argued that school uniforms did not address the causes of complex problems. They insisted that myriad factors were responsible for problems such as school attendance, academic achievement, inappropriate behavior, substance use, and dropouts (Brunsma & Rockquemore, 1998; Brunsma, 2004, 2006; Dowling-Sendor, 2002; Evans, 1996; Fast 2008; Newman, 2004). They demanded that they provide evidence about the genuine influence of uniforms.

EXAMINING ADVICE FROM IDEOLOGUES AND PRAGMATISTS

Researchers relied on different procedures to study somewhat similar problems. For example, they relied on distinct procedures to study automobile and motorcycle fatalities.

The automobile researchers considered numerous causes: vehicle size, safety equipment, road maintenance, weather conditions, traffic patterns, roadside distractions, road signals, traffic signs, driver attitudes, driver ages, driving regulations, alcohol, drugs, cell phones, police radar, and radar-evasion equipment.

In contrast, the motorcycle researchers restricted the scope of their investigation. Some of them looked at a single variable—the helmet. They also restricted the information that they shared with audiences.

Like the persons who examined vehicles, those who examined the schools made decisions about their investigations. Some of them broadly defined the scopes of studies and freely shared information. Others narrowly defined the scopes of studies and selectively released data.

The persons who examined the schools also had to make decisions about solutions. Some of them favored complex, comprehensive, and costly solutions; others favored simple, selective, and relatively inexpensive solutions.

Activity 5.1

You might decide to look for biases among researchers. You could examine researchers who studied non-scholastic and scholastic problems. You could use Table 5.1.

Table 5.1.   Non-Scholastic and Scholastic Problems

Group	Trait*			Rationale
	Trimming	Enhancing	Buttressing	
Automobile Deaths				
Motorcycle Deaths				
Ban on Gang Clothing				
School Uniforms				

*(1) Slight
(2) Moderate
(3) Robust

Table 5.1 identifies researchers. It lists four groups: those who respectively studied automobile deaths, motorcycle deaths, the ban on gang clothing in the schools, and the mandatory use of school uniforms.

This table allows you to indicate whether the researchers trimmed relevant data, enhanced select data, or presented data to buttress specific arguments.

Use numerals to complete the table. Choose the numeral *1* if the presence of a trait was slight. Use the numeral *2* if it was moderate and the numeral *3* if it was robust.

Finally, explain your selections. You could rely on the information in this chapter, the books that are cited in it, additional books, or your personal experiences.

Activity 5.2

You might wish to examine the behaviors of researchers from a different perspective. You might focus on those who endorsed relatively simple solutions to scholastic problems. You could use Table 5.2.

Table 5.2 identifies two groups: researchers who wished to ban gang clothing and those who wished to make school uniforms mandatory. Table 5.2 also allows you to select another group that recommended a relatively simple solution for scholastic problems. You can choose the third group by yourself, with another reader, or with a small group of readers.

To complete this table, consider whether groups trimmed relevant data, enhanced select data, or presented data to buttress specific arguments. Use the numerals in the legend of the table to indicate the degree to which these traits were present. Explain your responses.

Table 5.2. School Problems

Group	Trait*			Rationale
	Trimming	Enhancing	Buttressing	
Ban on Gang Clothing				
School Uniforms				
Other:				

*(1) Slight
(2) Moderate
(3) Robust

Activity 5.3

You might choose a distinct perspective from which to examine solutions to problems. You might want to hypothesize about the ways in which educational stakeholders reacted to them. You could use Table 5.3.

Table 5.3 lists two simple-to-implement solutions for complex scholastic problems. It lists the ban on gang clothing and the mandatory use of school uniforms. It gives you the chance to select another simple-to-implement solution to a complex problem. You can identify the third solution by yourself, with another reader, or with a small group of readers.

Table 5.3.   Reactions to Simple-to-Implement Practices

| Group | Practice* | | | Explanation |
	Ban on Gang Clothing	School Uniforms	Other:	
Parents				
Teachers				
Principals				
Conservative School Boards				
Liberal School Boards				

* (–) Low Support
 (–/+) Moderate Support
 (+) High Support

This table also identifies groups of educational stakeholders. It lists parents, teachers, principals, politically conservative school board members, and politically liberal school board members. Indicate each group's reaction to the proposals.

Use the symbol – to indicate that groups demonstrated a low degree of support for a proposed practice. Use the symbol –/+ for moderate support and the symbol + for high support. Finally, provide explanations.

SUMMARY

Researchers had to make difficult decisions about the variables that they would examine and the data that they would share. They sometimes trimmed relevant data, enhanced select observations, and presented information to buttress their preconceptions.

Chapter 6

Would German Philosophers Allow Animals in School?

If the doctor said to you, "You have a cold; here are three pills my buddy in Charlotte uses and he says they work," you would run out and find another doctor. . . . [but] somehow, in education, that approach is O.K.

—Roland Fryer [as quoted by Hernandez, 2008]

When philosophers and psychologists developed explanations for learning, they explicitly identified the theories on which they depended. When educators developed explanations for learning, some of them also identified theories. However, others referred to them implicitly. Still others ignored them altogether.

PHILOSOPHERS

Some eighteenth-century philosophers were idealists. Led by Immanuel Kant, a group of German idealists asked about the degree to which mental images resembled real objects. They discovered that this seemingly straightforward question was maddeningly complex.

The intricacy of the idealists' question became apparent when it was rephrased in different contexts. For example, assume that human beings evolved from much simpler life forms. Consider the situation that they would be in today had all of them acquired only four senses—smell, taste, hearing, and touch. If they could gather information just through these senses, what types of mental images could they form? If they never had acquired sight, could they incorporate color into their images?

One can regard the preceding situation from another perspective. Assume that humans are still evolving and that their destiny entails the acquisition of forty-seven senses. How will future creatures react when they look back on the efforts of their five-sensed precursors?

The eighteenth-century idealists contended that humans never could confirm whether mental images were distorted. They relied on a counterintuitive theory to explain their contentions (Guyer, 2006; Kuehn, 2001).

PSYCHOLOGISTS

Like philosophers, psychologists inquired about the nature of human knowledge and the conditions under which it was acquired. However, they assumed a distinctive viewpoint: they focused on extremely practical questions.

The behaviorists wished to demonstrate how persons solved everyday problems. To reduce their demonstrations to simple terms, they extracted insights from animal learning. They noted that animals learned efficiently when they had opportunities to earn rewards or avoid punishments (Bjork, 1993; O'Donohue & Ferguson, 2001).

B. F. Skinner and a group of behavioral psychologists investigated the ways in which animals reacted to different types of incentives. They also investigated the optimal schedules for administering incentives, the amount of learning that different types of incentives produced, and the persistence of that learning. After they had devised a theory to explain the ways in which animals learned, they generalized it to humans.

Skinner and his associates provided extensive and extremely practical advice about learning. They claimed that their advice could be applied to most human situations, including classroom learning (Skinner, 1968; Skinner & Epstein, 1982; Skinner & Krakower, 1968). They adjured educators to follow their recommendations.

Many educators were impressed by the practicality of this advice; they also were impressed by its familiarity. It seemed like most of them had implemented it even before they had heard about it from the psychologists.

EDUCATORS

When philosophers and psychologist gave advice about practical issues, they recognized that that their credibility hinged on theoretical assumptions. Anticipating that they would be asked about these assumptions, they explicitly elaborated them. Some of them elaborated intuitive theories; others developed counterintuitive theories. They then attempted to convince persons that their theories were reasonable.

Like philosophers and psychologists, educators were concerned about practical issues. After all, they dealt with instructing, disciplining, and assessing students. Like other scholars, they were pressed to disclose their theoretical assumptions.

Some educators carefully explained the theories on which they relied. Others explained them in somewhat casual fashions. Still others, who supposed that theoretical rationales were unnecessary, proffered exclusively practical information. Educators revealed their attitudes about theories on numerous occasions, such as when they were deliberating about standardized tests.

Some of the educators who used standardized tests explicitly acknowledged their dependence on the theory of the behavioral psychologists. Others assumed that persons would detect their implicit dependence on this theory. Still others, who had practical reasons for using tests, insisted that their practical reasons would suffice.

TESTS

Early teachers had numerous responsibilities. They personally developed curricula and instructed students. They also had to assess students. They assessed them by posing questions about essential information. They sometimes required them to respond in writing; they usually required them to respond orally (Giordano, 2005).

Practices

Critics noted that the early tests were unreliable. They judged that their value depended on the qualifications of the teachers who devised them. They pointed out that parents, employers, and government leaders, who did not have information about teachers, could not gauge the value of the tests that they administered. Although they had been disconcerted by this problem for decades, they became especially upset about it during World War I.

Wartime Tests

The World War I military leaders were flooded with draftees and recruits. They realized that they needed a way to rapidly and accurately assess them. Although they had access to school transcripts and diplomas, they dismissed them as unreliable. Suspecting that standardized tests would be more useful, they hired psychologists to custom-design exams for military applications.

Journalists informed the public that army psychologists were giving tests to millions of World War I soldiers. They also reported about the low scores that the soldiers were earning. They warned that poorly educated recruits were destabilizing the army and undermining the nation. They blamed teachers for ignoring this problem.

Enthusiasts claimed that standardization had helped prevent military and national tragedies. They claimed that they could solve additional problems, including problems in the schools. They noted that standardized tests, which were more objective than teacher-created exams, enabled the public to compare the progress of students in different classrooms, schools, cities, states, and regions. They judged that they provided a foundation for scholastic accountability.

Enthusiasts ascribed many additional advantages to standardized tests. They claimed that they saved time and money because they were simple to administer and easy to score. They added that they made sense for large districts because they were geared to the standardized curricula that these districts were implementing.

Enthusiasts claimed that standardized tests introduced valuable statistical procedures into the schools. They anticipated that these procedures would revise the shoddy manners in which educational problems had been investigated. They alleged that they could modernize the ways in which educators developed curricula, wrote textbooks, designed physical facilities, managed educational programs, identified weaknesses in student learning, and conducted instruction.

Tests as Incentives

Students always had been concerned about the ways in which their teachers evaluated them. Once they began to take standardized tests, they became concerned about the ways in which those tests evaluated them. They especially worried when test scores affected school activities, employment, or higher education.

Critics of the schools were aware that students worried about their performances on tests. They wished to use their concerns to raise academic achievement. However, they judged that the students were more concerned about the opinions of their teachers and school administrators than they were about their test scores.

Critics wondered how students would react if educators exhibited greater interest in standardized test scores. They wanted to increase the interests of teachers, principals, superintendents, and other school personnel. They were sure that they could increase the school personnel's interest if student test scores were used to evaluate them as well as their students.

School critics insisted that the scores that students earned on standardized tests were a legitimate way to evaluate teachers and school administrators. Nonetheless, they realized that the plan was controversial. They justified it by pointing to the similarities between this plan and those that businesspersons had implemented. Businesspersons used worker-productivity to evaluate laborers, and also used it to evaluate their supervisors and managers. They claimed that this procedure increased production, lowered expenses, and expanded profits.

High-Stakes Tests

Among the many groups of educational stakeholders that had demanded school reforms, businesspersons were one of the most vocal and persistent. They detected extraordinary opportunities to make changes during wartime.

Businesspersons were excited about the school-based campaigns of World War I. They praised them for reducing consumption and expanding production. They pointed out that the campaigns had enabled them to supply the Allied Powers with larger amounts of food, medicine, fuel, and war materiel (Giordano, 2003).

Frugal-minded critics were another group of educational stakeholders who demanded school reforms. During World War I, they agreed with the businesspersons about the need to reduce the public's consumption; they also wanted to reduce the government's spending. Concerned about unnecessary scholastic spending, they urged legislators and community leaders to cut school expenditures and reallocate the money that they saved (Giordano, 2005).

Critics of the schools complained that even poorly performing schools had excessive budgets. They proposed to eliminate this waste by linking budgets with productivity. They explained that students' test scores were objective gauges of school productivity. They then had another idea for promoting efficiency: they wanted to link the salaries of teachers and school administrators to students' test scores (Giordano, 2009).

Throughout the twentieth century, educational critics tried to make school reforms. Many of them were impressed by the bonuses that business executives had used to motivate workers and managers. They hoped to find a comparable incentive for teachers and school administrators. Unwilling to pay bonuses, they made operating budgets into incentives.

Educators were outraged by attempts to make operating budgets into incentives. Searching for a pejorative term, they referred to the practice as "high-stakes" testing. Although they conceded that this type of testing could stimulate competition, they insisted that it was faulty.

Educators argued that high-stakes testing was flawed because it made them accountable for students over whom they had limited influence. They argued that they had relatively little influence on the test scores of students who were recent immigrants, who had disabilities, or who were impoverished. They predicted that talented and hard-working educators would be penalized if they taught significant numbers of these students. They added that they would be penalized even though they were serving the students who had the greatest educational needs (Giordano, 2005).

Theory

Some teachers told students about the explicit expectations that they set for them. They lectured them about the consequences of misbehavior; they published policies about the penalties for academic failure. Other teachers expressed their expectations implicitly: they expressed them by ringing bells, convening assemblies, setting rules, prescribing common learning materials, and implementing lockstep curricula.

Teachers punished students who did not meet their expectations. Some of them used relatively mild punishments: they frowned, scolded, canceled recess, or assigned extra homework to them. Others went further: they shook, pulled, slapped, struck, or expelled students.

Teachers used punishments when students did not meet their expectations; they used rewards when they met them. In fact, many of them intentionally paired punishments and rewards. While they were frowning at some children, they were smiling at others. While they were relegating some children to corners, they were moving others to the fronts of classrooms. While they were demoting some, they were advancing others. While they were withholding school liberties from some, they were bestowing extra privileges on others.

Before teachers could punish or reward students, they had to assess whether they were meeting expectations. In instances of student deportment, assessment was relatively straightforward. In cases of academic achievement, assessment was more complicated. Even attempts to explain the rationale for academic assessment were complicated.

SUNGLASSES FOR READING

During the 1980s, Helen Irlen was concerned about persons with disabilities. She came up with a peculiar remedial practice: wearing sunglasses. Even though she conceded that the practice was simple, she claimed that it had astonishing effects (Irlen, 1991).

Irlen claimed that peering through colored lenses while reading helped students with visual irregularities; she added that it also helped those with dyslexia. Even though she stunned many persons with these announcements, she went on to make claims that were more startling.

Irlen claimed that the use of colored lenses alleviated psychological abnormalities. She referred to examples in which it had eased and sometimes cured these problems. She alleged that it also helped persons with headaches, concussions, traumatic brain injuries, and other medical ailments.

Irlen claimed the use of colored lenses helped persons with still more types of problems. She asserted that it helped persons with mild learning disabilities such as attention deficit disorder. She claimed that it helped persons with profound learning problems such as autism. She added that it even helped students who were progressing normally in school but who wished to do better. She made the same claim about students who were gifted but who wished to achieve at higher levels.

Practices

Irlen (1998) wished to be sure that potential clients understood some of the problems that her remedial practices addressed and the ways in which it affected them. Therefore, she referred them to a website with computer simulations on it.

In one simulation, several lines of animated print intermingled in seesaw-like patterns. In another case, animated letters leaned from left to right in a pulsing rhythm. In still another case, a vibrant display began to fade.

Irlen alleged that wearing sunglasses during reading cured problems such as those that she had depicted on her website. She even devised a practical demonstration to reveal the way in which the treatment worked. After directing clients to a webpage on which a special palette of colors was displayed, she encouraged them to select one of those colors.

Irlen explained that selecting the color blue on the palette would change the webpage's white background into a blue background. She anticipated that members of her audience would have less difficulty reading the information on the website once the color behind the text had been changed. She hoped that they quickly would comprehend why her remedial practices were effective.

Irlen attempted to refine her practices. For example, she predicted that some persons would find the sunglasses uncomfortable. She offered a suggestion: they could attach the sunglasses to a special visor. She informed them that they could purchase visors from her.

Irlen anticipated that some individuals would not be satisfied with the visors. She had another useful suggestion. They could avoid the glasses altogether and place sheets of translucent, colored film over their reading materials. As with the visors, they could purchase the sheets from her.

Theory

Irlen anticipated that consumers would demand that she identify the theory of learning on which her practices were based. She was prepared; she informed them that "brain research at the cellular level" provided a "plausible" basis for her practices.

Some clients were impressed with Irlen's curt assurance. They felt that the alleged grounding in neurological research gave them the information that they needed to feel confident about her practices.

Entrepreneurial businesspersons, clinicians, and educators were impressed by the way in which Irlen had connected learning practices to neurological research. They made similar claims about their own practices and products. They convened workshops, organized conventions, wrote books, established websites, and started clinics to promote their services and materials.

Scores of authors decided that they would underscore connections between educational practices and neurological theory. They highlighted these connections when they designated titles for their books. They selected titles such as *Brain Research and Childhood Education, A Brain-Compatible Approach to Reaching Middle and High School Students,* and *Using the Brain's Natural Learning Process to Create Today's Curriculum* (Bergen & Coscia, 2001; Philp, 2007; Smilkstein, 2003).

ANIMALS IN SCHOOL

Throughout time, domestic animals have provided companionship to humans. As an example, the dogs that lived on farms and ranches were companions to their owners. However, these dogs also were workers: they pulled carts, steered herds, and protected flocks from predators.

In addition to serving as companions and workers, dogs sometimes had specialized duties. Those that accompanied persons with disabilities were assigned extraordinarily specialized responsibilities.

Practices

Dogs traditionally were assigned to individuals who were visually impaired. Members of the public understood the rationale for this practice; they realized that the dogs had senses that compensated for those that the owners lacked. However, dogs provided other types of help to persons with disabilities.

Some dogs helped persons who had convulsions. Referred to as seizure dogs, these animals came to the assistance of owners when they were immobilized. Some of them sat protectively over the fallen humans; others barked, fetched caregivers, or activated electronic alarms (Armstrong & Botzler, 2003; Brown & Strong, 2001; Spencer, 2007).

Seizure dogs had demonstrated unusual sensitivity to their owners' conditions. Some of them detected convulsions before humans could observe them. Others detected the early stages of convulsions even before the victims were aware of them. In both cases, they gave owners the opportunity to take precautionary steps.

Enthusiasts gave additional examples in which dogs used their rarified senses to help humans. They pointed to cases in which they had helped medical doctors. They noted that dogs had been able to recognize the peculiar odors associated with lung and breast cancer (McNamara, 2006).

Although some persons assigned practical roles to domestic animals, others gave them different sorts of roles (Allen, 1985). Persons who ascribed social and emotional characteristics to animals made them into intimate companions. Older persons who were lonely communicated their feelings to pets and insisted that their pets reciprocated (Thomas, 1996).

Some persons maintained that pets changed the perspectives from which they viewed their lives; others maintained that they mystically influenced their lives. Persons who ascribed mystical traits to pets substantiated their views with personal testimonials (Schoen, 2001).

Theory

Critics were skeptical about animal-assisted learning. They pointed out that the interactions between humans and pets were difficult to discern, categorize, and interpret. They challenged the ways in which the enthusiasts had interpreted these interactions.

Even though they conceded that the relationships between humans and pets were ambiguous and complicated, the enthusiasts believed that their impressions were accurate. For example, they insisted that human-pet relationships were therapeutic (Abdill & Juppé, 1997; Crawford & Pomerinke, 2003; Fine, 2000; Graham, 2000). They substantiated this impression with the numerous reports about animals that had helped persons with physical or emotional problems (Fine & Eisen, 2008; Pichot & Coulter, 2007; Snyder & Lindquist, 1998).

The enthusiasts for animal-assisted learning easily gathered supporters for some of their initiatives. They found many persons who agreed that therapy animals provided practical help to individuals with physical disabilities.

However, they had a more difficult time finding persons who agreed that animals could discharge subtle responsibilities, such as providing emotional and social support to hospital patients.

Because they were convinced that animals could help patients, enthusiasts urged critics to allow them into medical facilities. Because they also were convinced that animals could help students with disabilities, they urged critics to allow them into educational facilities (Chandler, 2005; Devinsky, Schachter, & Pacia, 2005; Pavlides, 2008).

Enthusiasts wished to recruit persons to support the expansion of animal-assisted learning. Because their most ardent supporters had trained therapy animals, they exhorted all pet owners to follow their lead. They counseled them to train pets, make first-hand observations, and provide testimonials about their powers (Burch, 1996). They even exhorted children to transform pets into therapy animals (Kent, 2003; Frydenborg, 2006; Murray, 2009; Oliver, 1999; Rylant & Schindler, 1985).

When school administrators and teachers were lobbied to invite animals into the schools, some of them complied. The sympathizers detected the implicit theoretical foundation on which the practices were based. However, others resisted. The critics raised questions about the practicality, expense, and liabilities of animal-assisted learning. They also posed questions about the theory on which it was based.

EXAMINING THEORETICAL ADVICE

Philosophers and psychologists made theoretical assumptions about knowledge and learning. They explicitly identified their assumptions.

Educators also made assumptions about knowledge and learning. Some of them followed the lead of the philosophers and psychologists. However, others referred to theories implicitly. Still others ignored theories and relied instead on exclusively practical rationales.

Activity 6.1

You might wish to analyze theories. You could analyze the degree to which scholars acknowledged their theoretical assumptions. You could rely on Table 6.1.

Table 6.1 identifies the proponents of five initiatives: Kant's philosophy, Skinner's psychology, high-stakes testing, reading with sunglasses, and animal-assisted learning. Indicate the degree to which the members of each group identified their theoretical assumptions.

Use letters to complete this table. Use the letter *E* if the members of a group explicitly identified theoretical assumptions. Use the letter *I* if they made implicit theoretical assumptions. Use the letter *D* if they disregarded theory.

As the final step, explain your responses. You could provide explanations on the basis of the information in this chapter. You also could rely on the books that are cited in this chapter, additional books, or your personal experiences.

Table 6.1. Theoretical Assumptions by Scholars

Group	Assumption*	Explanation
Kant		
Skinner		
Testing		
Sunglasses		
Animals		

*(E) Explicit
(I) Implicit
(D) Disregarded

Activity 6.2

You could guide your analysis of theories in another direction. For example, you might analyze the ways in which different groups reacted to them. You could use Table 6.2.

Table 6.2 identifies four educational initiatives: those that respectively were associated with Skinner, high-stakes testing, reading with sunglasses, and therapy animals. The proponents of these initiatives may have addressed theories explicitly, implicitly, or not at all.

This table also identifies some of the educational stakeholders that responded to the initiatives. It lists teachers, parents, school administrators, politicians, and businesspersons.

Use symbols to complete this table. Use the symbol – if a group of stakeholders expressed low support for the ways which enthusiasts addressed theories. Use the symbol –/+ to indicate moderate support and the symbol + to indicate high support. Explain your selections.

Table 6.2. Reactions to Educational Theories

Group	Initiative*				Explanation
	Skinner	Testing	Sunglasses	Animals	
Teachers					
Parents					
School Administrators					
Politicians					
Business-persons					

* (–) Low Support
(–/+) Moderate Support
(+) High Support

Activity 6.3

You might wish to analyze theories from still another perspective. You could analyze the ways in which groups reacted to implicit theories. You could use Table 6.3.

Table 6.3 gives you opportunities to identify the reactions of several groups. It lists five groups: teachers, parents, school administrators, politicians, and businesspersons.

Analyze the ways in which the groups reacted to the implicit theory that was associated with therapy animals; also analyze their reactions to the implicit theory associated with another educational incident. You can select the second incident. You can select it by yourself, with another reader, or with a small group of readers.

Use the symbols in the table's legend to complete this table. As a final step, provide explanations for the symbols that you select.

Table 6.3. Reactions to Implicit Theories

Group	Theory* Animals	Theory* Other:	Explanation
Teachers			
Parents			
School Admin- istrators			
Politicians			
Business- persons			

* (–) Low Support
(–/+) Moderate Support
(+) High Support

Chapter 6

SUMMARY

When scholars were pressed to rationalize their views, some of them adduced intuitive theories; others adduced counterintuitive theories. Skinner, the twentieth-century psychologist, presented an intuitive theory. Kant, the eighteenth-century philosopher, presented a counterintuitive theory.

When educators were asked to provide theoretical rationales for learning practices, some of them complied. Others responded indirectly. Still others ignored the requests.

Chapter 7

Should Educators Crowdsource?

The labor [one needs for crowdsourcing] isn't always free, but it costs a lot less than paying traditional employees.

—Jeff Howe, 2006

Individuals relied on their personal intuitions to answer questions about popular culture, health, and politics. They sometimes relied on them to answer questions about education.

POPULISTS

Businesspersons needed information to help them make decisions. They asked professionals in advertising, marketing, and branding to help them. Although most of them were pleased by this collaboration, some of them searched for an alternative.

Businesspersons were confident that they would find an alternative way to make strategic decisions; they believed that they would find a way that was practical, tested, and inexpensive. They were optimistic because numerous approaches were available.

Persons had studied decision making in business for decades. However, they had studied it in other contexts for a much longer period. In fact, Plato had studied it in ancient Greece. In his most famous treatise, *The Republic,* he evaluated the advantages and disadvantages of populist decision making.

Like the ancient Greeks, later analysts were fascinated by populist decision making. Scholars and politicians deliberated about it when they implemented national constitutions. The scholars focused on the theoretical aspects of constitutions; the politicians focused on the practical aspects (Tierney, 2004).

Persons have continued to discuss the merits of populist decision making. Many of them have concluded that its advantages outweighed its disadvantages. The enthusiasts advised professionals to employ it in fields such as government, medicine, education, and business (Ariely, 2008; Buchanan & Brock, 1989; Eckel, 2006; Miller, 2008; Morcol, 2007; Moss, 2007; Surowiecki, 2004).

Businesspersons

Businesspersons were intrigued when scholars encouraged them to elicit information directly from the public. Some of them were interested because this recommendation entailed a chance to save money. Others were interested because the advice was unexpected. They had anticipated that the scholars, who were experts, would urge them to rely on advice from other experts.

When modern businesspersons decided to experiment with populist decision making, they gave it a new name: *crowdsourcing* (Howe, 2006; Barrett, 2007). They soon detected multiple opportunities to use it. For example, they detected opportunities to use it in the film industry.

Film executives were concerned about the declining numbers of persons who were attending movies. They speculated that the ways some films ended had made audiences reluctant to return to the cinema. Traditionally, the executives had allowed writers, directors, and producers to select film endings. However, they worried that they had jeopardized the studios' profits with their endings.

The film executives asked their production personnel to create several endings for each new film. They then assembled test audiences, exhibited versions of films with different endings, and asked audiences to express their preferences. They used the advice from the test audiences to pick the endings for films (Marich, 2005).

Film executives were not the only businesspersons who experimented with crowdsourcing. Executives in other fields employed it for numerous ventures. They relied on it extensively in marketing and advertising. In some cases, they confirmed the effectiveness of the approaches that they currently were using; in other cases, they looked for new approaches (Rosen, 2000).

Conspiracy Theorists

Writing in ancient Greece, Plato had noted that a democracy significantly empowered members of the general populace. Worried about this enormous power, he predicted that members of the public would misuse it. He predicted that they would inappropriately influence government leaders and scholars.

Proponents of democratic decision making demonstrated their prowess at propagating and defending information on numerous occasions. For example, they demonstrated it when they propounded conspiracy theories. Even though they lacked evidence to validate these theories, they were able to attract supporters.

Popular Culture

Conspiracy theorists turned their attention to multiple types of incidents. They sometimes focused on incidents that were part of popular culture (Birchall, 2006). For example, they maintained that dead celebrities were alive. They insisted that Elvis Presley, the American entertainer, did not die in 1977. To substantiate this contention, they referred to witnesses. The witnesses reported seeing Presley after his alleged death; they reported seeing him at convenience stores, restaurants, and gasoline stations.

Although some conspiracy theorists maintained that dead celebrities were alive, others insisted that living persons had died. For example, they claimed that Paul McCartney, the British entertainer, had died during the 1970s. To substantiate this allegation, they identified a Beatles recording which, when played backwards, contained allusions to McCartney's death. Although skeptics could not detect these allusions, they could not persuade the conspiracy theorists to abandon their contention.

Skeptics had another reason for challenging the allegations about McCartney's death; the singer appeared in public every day. The conspiracy theorists were not phased; they insisted that a clever impersonator had taken the place of the deceased Beatle.

Politics

Although some conspiracy theorists focused on entertainment and popular culture, others concentrated on politics. As an example, they disputed the 1969 moon landing by United States astronauts. When they were challenged with video recordings, they dismissed them as simulations. They explained that government leaders had political reasons for arranging the simulations ("Did We Land," 2009).

Conspiracy theorists devised political explanations for the deaths of numerous persons: they came up with explanations for the deaths of Marilyn Monroe, John F. Kennedy, and Princess Dianna (Emery, 2008).

Conspiracy theorists claimed that American politicians regularly exploited events to advance their political interests. They accused them of committing crimes to influence elections (Bugliosi, 2007; Freeman & Bleifuss, 2006). They accused them of orchestrating the 9/11 attacks, or at least allowing them to occur, to advance partisan plans (Freedman, 2008).

Motives

Persons speculated about the motives of the individuals who created, propagated, and defended conspiracy theories (Parker & Parish, 2001; Ronson, 2002; York, 2005). They noted that these individuals sometimes were devious. They found examples in which political operatives promoted conspiracy theories to embarrass rival politicians.

Conspiracy theorists described themselves as intellectually independent individuals who distrusted the political establishment and the mainstream media. However, analysts disagreed. Some of the analysts depicted the conspiracy theorists as intellectually insecure persons who wished to blame others for the troubling situations that they had helped create (Marche, 2009).

Still other political analysts characterized conspiracy theorists as persons who were searching for intellectually and emotionally uncomplicated explanations. They judged that they were drawn to fringe movements because the persons in these movements claimed to have certain answers to complex questions (Parker & Parish, 2001).

Some analysts depicted political conspiracy theorists as ideologically malleable. They took a point of view that was similar to that of Eric Hoffer. In the middle of the twentieth century, Hoffer had written a controversial book about ideologues. Referring to ideologues as true believers, he depicted them as individuals who were emotionally predisposed to mass movements (Hoffer, 1951).

Hoffer hypothesized that groups of true believers were distinguished only by circumstantial differences. He explained that the true believers who lived in totalitarian countries joined the anti-democratic movements that were prevalent in their locales. Conversely, true believers who lived in democratic countries joined anti-totalitarian movements solely because these were common in their communities.

Medical Consumers

Persons who distrusted journalists turned to political fringe movements. Those who distrusted the medical establishment turned to other types of fringe movements—those that promoted alternative health practices. Some persons used alternative practices to supplement traditional medicines; others used them exclusively.

Advocates for alternative health practices sometimes tried to recruit adherents with alarmist rhetoric. For example, they accused doctors, medical researchers, and traditional health professionals of being poorly informed and dishonest (Bausell, 2007; Trudeau, 2004). They implored persons to avoid traditional medical practitioners and rely instead on those who provided alternative care (Carper, 1997; Gottlieb, 2000; Haugen, 2008; Larson, 2007; Mackenzie & Rakel, 2006; Whorton, 2002).

The proponents of alternative health practices made suggestions for promoting wellness and curing disease. In fact, they made scores of suggestions. Some of them encouraged exposure to heat while others encouraged exposure to cold. Some of them recommended envelopment in light while others recommended envelopment in darkness.

Some proponents of alternative health practices encouraged persons to ingest herbs, spices, vitamins, and special foods. Others encouraged them to use magnets, crystals, minerals, meditation, relaxation, biofeedback, hypnotherapy, massage, chiropractic, acupressure, acupuncture, tai chi, yoga, stretching, balancing, martial arts, and dance.

Enthusiasts had multiple reasons for subscribing to alternative health practices. Some subscribed because they had lost confidence in traditional health practices. Some subscribed because of experimental evidence. Others subscribed because of testimonials from associates, friends, family members, and neighbors. Still others subscribed because of their own experiences.

Physicians and medical specialists had questions about alternative health practices. They noted that their own research challenged the studies on which the alternative practices were based. They wondered whether enthusiasts had been misled by placebos.

Medical researchers were sure that placebos could confuse consumers. They confirmed this conviction with experiments. In their studies, they gave patients either pills with medication or pills without it; however, they did not reveal to the patients which type of treatment they received. Researchers concluded that persons had been deceived after they insisted that the ineffective placebos relieved symptoms (Moerman, 2002; Thompson, 2005).

EDUCATIONAL EXPERTS AND POPULISTS

During the nineteenth century, children stayed away from the schools and worked instead. Many of them worked in their homes or on the streets; others worked at docks, restaurants, factories, farms, and mines. Some early twentieth-century community leaders, such as those in Chicago, wanted to lure children from workplaces and into the schools.

When they decided that they would open Chicago's schools to working children, community leader were aware that they had to deal with formidable challenges. To reduce those challenges, they appointed principals, hired teachers, erected buildings, landscaped playgrounds, arranged transportation, purchased equipment, ordered textbooks, developed curricula, and assembled operating budgets.

Even though they planned carefully, the Chicago leaders later realized that they should have shown greater foresight. After the new students had arrived, their teachers were not prepared for those who spoke multiple languages, came from impoverished homes, wore inappropriate clothing, carried infectious diseases, were malnourished, suffered from poor health, and had mental disabilities.

Chicago's leaders were unable to deal with many of the new students that they had admitted into their schools. They turned to experts.

Experts Examine Sick Students

Chicago's community leaders approached a variety of experts for help. They approached social workers, court officials, and police officers. They also asked for help from optometrists, nurses, doctors, dentists, and healthcare experts.

The experts analyzed the problems in the schools; they also examined the ways in which those problems were affecting students. Some of the problems affected only select students. For example, the students who arrived at school hungry suffered in ways that were regrettable and even inhumane; nonetheless, they did not affect their classmates. The students with contagious diseases had a different type of impact.

Health experts warned that the children who resided in Chicago's disease-infested slums would infect students who were well. They advised school administrators to take several steps: hire fulltime nurses, inoculate students, and provide healthcare.

The recommendations from experts were expensive to put into practice. Unable to implement them extensively, community leaders did not reduce the enormous health problems in their schools. They looked for alternative, reasonably priced solutions. They asked school administrators, teachers, and parents to give them advice.

Populists Examine Sick Students

When school administrators, teachers, and parents were asked about ways to check the spread of disease in the schools, they relied on their intuitions. For example, they relied on their intuitions when they conjectured that the healthy students were contracting diseases from infected textbooks.

The educators and parents again relied on their intuitions when they devised a solution to the problems created by germ-infested books. They urged community leaders to shorten the cycle for textbook purchases. However, they did not anticipate that this process, which was costly, would be implemented widely (Giordano, 2003).

The persons who were concerned about germs on books tried to come up with inexpensive plans. For example, they began to sanitize old textbooks. Some of them wiped book covers with disinfectants. Others gathered grocery bags, cut them up, and made paper jackets for the books. They were disappointed when these steps did not reduce the health problems.

Educators and parents continued to look for inexpensive ways to guard students' health. After they noticed that the students were particularly unhealthy during the winter season, they believed that they had found an opportunity to make a difference. They reasoned that the students' classrooms, which were turned into germ-ridden hothouses in winter, could be disinfected by Chicago's frigid air.

The educators and parents decided to test their hunch. They began by extinguishing the fires in the school furnaces. Although they told the students to remain at their desks and continue to study, they directed them to put on their boots, coats, hats, scarves, and gloves. They then opened the windows of their classrooms.

Intrepid teachers were not satisfied with opening classroom windows: they carried desks, chairs, textbooks, and equipment onto their buildings' glacial rooftops. They then taught their students in the fresh-air classrooms that they had improvised. Although some students objected, their teachers had a ready response: discomfort was a reasonable price to pay for health.

Proponents of the fresh-air classrooms hoped to cure ailing students and safeguard their peers. However, they eventually realized that frozen students were not healthier than warm ones. They made their students squeal with delight when they closed the windows, hauled the furniture off of the rooftops, rekindled the furnaces, and allowed them to remove their outdoor apparel.

Experts Examine Poor Students

During the early years of the twentieth century, educators welcomed many new children into the schools. As one example, they welcomed children with severe health problems. However, they were concerned about children with numerous other problems. They worried particularly about those who lived in poverty.

Early educators were concerned that the problems that impoverished children faced in their homes and neighborhoods would influence them in school. Although these problems affected the children's own academic progress, they also affected that of their classmates.

Like the children who came to school a century ago, impoverished children continue to suffer today; they continue to suffer in their homes, neighborhoods, and schools. They continue to suffer personally; they continue to affect their peers. They even affect their teachers, who worry whether these children can deal with their physical, social, economic, emotional, and academic problems.

Like earlier teachers, current teachers have asked experts for advice about impoverished children. Experts responded with advice about the optimal way to teach reading (Barone, 2006; Flood & Anders, 2005; Graves, Van Den Broek, & Taylor, 1996; Lapp, 2004; Neuman, 2008). They also gave advice about the best ways to teach other academic subjects (Kincheloe, 2007; Lewin-Benham, 2006; Ohanian, 2001).

Some experts followed a different tack when they were formulating advice about impoverished children; they advised teachers and school administrators to be aware of the broad social, political, and economic problems affecting them. They extracted this advice from the research literature in sociology, economics, and political science (Kincheloe & Steinberg, 2007; Rothstein, 1994). Some of them advised educators to look for ways in which urban environments accentuated the problems that accompanied poverty (Ravitch & Viteritti, 1997).

Although some experts gave advice to school personnel, others gave advice about them. They encouraged community leaders and school board members to hire teachers and school administrators who could interact effectively with impoverished children. To assist them, they listed the traits of model educators (Bullough, 2001; Lyman & Villani, 2004).

Some experts gave advice to politicians rather than educators. They advised them that impoverished children had difficulty in school because of learning gaps; they explained that these gaps resulted from the differences between their experiences and those of other children. They urged politicians to find the funds to help educators bridge these gaps (Silver & Silver, 1991; Slavin & Madden, 2001; Stein, 2004; Stern, 2003).

Federal politicians funneled hundreds of billions of dollars into early learning programs. They then convened conferences, conducted congressional hearings, and circulated reports to publicize the programs that they had established (e.g., United States Department of Education, 1989; United States House of Representatives Committee on Education and the Workforce, 2003; United States Senate Committee on Health, Education, Labor, and Pensions, 2005).

Politicians collaborated with experts to solve educational problems. However, they collaborated with numerous other groups. In fact, they frequently listened intently to these other groups.

EDUCATIONAL CROWDSOURCING

Politicians wished to see the schools improve. They were convinced that improved schools would raise the quality of living for citizens. Nonetheless, they had an additional reason to promote school improvement: they needed revenue.

Local government leaders needed money to fund crime prevention, firefighting, sanitation, road construction, parks, recreation, and healthcare. National leaders needed revenue to fund domestic, international, and defense programs. The politicians explained that educated citizens, who were more prosperous than non-educated citizens, increased governmental as well as personal assets.

Politicians were convinced that the prosperity of their constituents and the fate of their nation were connected to education. They asked school stakeholders for advice about improving education.

Stakeholders

When politicians resolved to gather populist advice, they had to designate the school stakeholders that they would consult. They had little difficulty recognizing leaders from business, the military, and religion as key stakeholders.

Business leaders were concerned about the schools for multiple reasons. They relied on them to educate workers and managers. They relied on them to prepare consumers for their products and services. They relied on them to purchase the equipment, textbooks, curricular materials, and standardized tests that they produced. They relied on them for opportunities to construct school buildings, athletic facilities, and playgrounds (Giordano, 2003).

Just as businesspersons depended on the schools to prepare workers, military leaders depended on them to prepare soldiers. During peaceful times, they were able to recruit persons selectively; during wartime, they were less fortunate. In fact, they were dismayed by the level to which they had lowered their standards during World War I. They adjured the school administrators to improve education. They repeated this adjuration throughout the twentieth century (Giordano, 2004, 2005).

Religious leaders also were concerned about the schools. They were convinced that the members of their churches and synagogues would attain spiritually full lives if they read inspirational books: the *Bible, Tanakh, Book of Mormon,* sermons, or prayers. They insisted that the schools nurture the prerequisite skills.

Parents

Although numerous groups wished to advise politicians about the schools, parents were at the front of the procession. Beginning in the colonial era, they had been concerned about the schools. They had demonstrated their concerns by placing sustained pressure on politicians (Cutler, 2000).

Parents had diverse reasons for pressuring politicians to improve the schools. Financially established parents depended on the schools to help their children rival or eclipse their own success. Parents with meager wealth depended on them for a different reason: they wanted their children to avoid hardship, poverty, and disease.

Parents from racial minority groups wanted the schools to create opportunities for their children. They wanted them to help their children progress through elementary school, high school, and college. They wanted them to help combat discrimination, injustice, and oppression.

Parents who recently immigrated to the United States expected the schools to instruct their children about the language, government, economy, customs, culture, and traditions of their new country. They also expected the schools to give their children the academic skills that they needed to become responsible, prosperous, and happy citizens.

Politicians Crowdsource Parents

During the 1970s, the members of Congress enacted legislation to reorganize special education (Education for All Handicapped Children Act, 1975). Within this legislation, they acknowledged the critical role of parents. They specified that parents should collaborate with school personnel to create custom-tailored educational programs.

The legislators who voted for the Education for All Handicapped Children Act affirmed the rights of parents whose children had disabilities (Giordano, 2007). Other legislators passed regulations, restrictions, and laws to clarify the roles, rights, and responsibilities of a wider range of parents. They explicitly affirmed the rights of parents who represented females, bilingual learners, and students from racial minority groups (Giordano, 2009).

Educators Crowdsource Parents

Parents were frustrated when school administrators ignored their advice. Some of them responded by sending their children to private schools; others taught them at home (Gaither, 2008; Princiotta, Bielick, & Chapman, 2006; Rivero, 2008). Although irritated parents could pull their children out of the schools, some of them responded in a different way: they became less involved.

Educators were concerned about the ways that uninvolved parents affected children. They noted that they influenced them academically; they noted that they also influenced them physically, socially, and emotionally. They resolved to regain their attention. However, they did not anticipate the enormity of this challenge.

Educators assumed that parents lost interest because they were disappointed in the schools. They eventually detected many other reasons. For example, parents lost interest because of the difficult situations that they were facing in their lives. Those who were dealing with divorces paid less attention to their children's education (Jeynes, 2002). Those who were depressed, drug dependent, alcoholic, or emotionally disturbed paid less attention as well (Berger, 2007).

When educators observed parents losing interest in education, they suspected that the parents might be confronting difficult personal challenges. They looked for clues with which to confirm their suspicions (Coleman, 1991). In addition to looking for clues about the parents, educators looked for clues about the parents' interactions with their children. They examined whether the parents were clothing, feeding, and attending to the health of their children.

As educators investigated children who were neglected, they were shocked by the frequency with which they had disabilities. They wondered whether the children's disabilities had become life-disrupting circumstances not only for them but also for other members of their families (Cimera, 2007; Kroth, Edge, & Kroth, 1997; Siegel, 2003; Taylor, 2004).

EXAMINING EXPERT AND POPULIST ADVICE

Early businesspersons needed information about consumers. They needed to know details about them, the types of advertisements to which they responded, and the products that they purchased. They asked marketing experts to help.

Although some businesspersons turned to experts, others crowdsourced by gathering information directly from consumers. They then decided whether to retain, alter, or abandon products and the ways that they promoted them.

Politicians, who were impressed by the crowdsourcing, used this technique to extract information from voters. Educators, who also were impressed, began to employ it with their constituents.

Educators easily could crowdsource some constituents. They had ready access to the healthcare providers, psychologists, social workers, court officers, and other professionals who worked in the schools. However, they had greater difficulty reaching the government leaders, businesspersons, military leaders, religious leaders, and other individuals who had stakes in the schools but who associated with them indirectly.

Activity 7.1

You might wish to hypothesize about the ways in which expert and populist information influenced groups. You could use Table 7.1.

Table 7.1 concentrates on three groups: conspiracy theorists, early advocates for poor students, and recent advocates for poor students.

Use numerals to complete this table. Use the numeral *1* if expert information had a low impact on a group. Use the numeral *2* for moderate impact and the numeral *3* for high impact. Use the same numerals to identify the impact of populist information.

Table 7.1.　Experts and Populists

Group	Information	Impact*	Rationale
Conspiracy Theorists	Expert		
	Populist		
Early Advocates for Poor Students	Expert		
	Populist		
Recent Advocates for Poor Students	Expert		
	Populist		

* (1) Low
 (2) Moderate
 (3) High

As a final step, explain your designations. You could rely on the information in this chapter, the books that are cited in it, additional books, or your personal experiences.

Activity 7.2

You could analyze the impact of populist information in another way. For example, you could analyze the ways in which different groups reacted to it. You could use Table 7.2.

Table 7.2 identifies five groups: teachers, parents, school administrators, members of the general public, and politicians. It gives you chances to indicate the ways in which these groups reacted to the populist information that was linked to conspiracy theories, the plight of poor children in the early schools, and the plight of poor children in the current schools.

Table 7.2. Reactions to Populists

Group	Populist Information*			Explanation
	Conspiracy Theories	*Poor Children— Early Schools*	*Poor Children— Current Schools*	
Teachers				
Parents				
School Admin- istrators				
General Public				
Politicians				

* (1) Low Support
 (2) Moderate Support
 (3) High Support

Use the numerals in the legend to complete the table. Finally, explain your reasons for the numerals that you selected.

Activity 7.3

You might wish to examine several incidents in which expert and populist information influenced the schools. You could use Table 7.3.

Table 7.3 gives you the chances to identify the expert and populist information associated with three recent school initiatives. It lists two of these initiatives: helping poor students and empowering parents. It allows you to designate the third initiative. You can designate the third initiative by yourself, with another reader, or with a small group of readers.

Table 7.3.   Experts and Populists Affect Current Education Issues

	Information				
Initiative	Expert	Impact*	Populist	Impact*	Rationale
Helping Poor Students					
Empowering Parents					
Other:					

* (1) Low
  (2) Moderate
  (3) High

To complete this table, indicate the degree to which expert and populist information influenced the groups that were associated with each initiative. Use the numerals in the legend. Finally, explain your selections.

SUMMARY

Members of the public sometimes concluded that expert recommendations were invalid or impractical. Relying on their own intuitions and experiences, they came up with recommendations of their own.

Chapter 8

Do Urban Legends Influence Educators?

There are no documented cases of contamination of Halloween candy, but the media and police issue warnings year after year.

—Tom Harris, 2001

Contrarians made unusual allegations. They were confident about them even though they lacked corroborative evidence; they remained confident even when they confronted contradictory evidence. They behaved in the same fashion when they made allegations about education.

CONTRARIANS

Contrarians provided unusual explanations for numerous incidents. Because their opinions were eccentric, they attracted attention. Some of their most widely publicized opinions were referred to as urban legends. In spite of this restrictive term, the legends concerned incidents that had transpired in both urban and non-urban locales (Brunvand, 1999, 2004; Genge, 2000; Roeper, 2008).

Some urban legends were particularly long-lived. For example, the stories of alligators in sewers endured for decades. According to these stories, tourists from the Northeast and the Midwest captured young Florida alligators, adopted them, and brought them to their city neighborhoods. After they had tired of these pets, they flushed them down their toilets. However, the pets survived. They grew into giant predators and roamed the sewers of Boston, Philadelphia, Cleveland, and other non-tropical cities (Emery, 2008).

Another urban legend concerned the architectural restrictions on the observation deck of the Empire State Building. The purveyors of this legend explained that coins thrown from the top of this New York City structure acquired enough force to bury themselves into the skulls of the persons passing on the sidewalks. They claimed that the restrictions on the deck became necessary after miscreants made it the launch site for their pennies (Stossel & Binkley, 2007).

Unlike the legends about alligators and skyscrapers, some tales did not have distinctive connections to cities. The proponents of one urban legend reported on an unglamorous formula for a trendy soft drink: they contended that prune juice was the primary ingredient of Dr. Pepper (Mikkelson & Mikkelson, 2007).

The proponents of another legend argued that food spilled onto soiled surfaces would remain germ-free for five seconds. They advised waiters and cooks to serve the food that had dropped onto floors—provided that they had retrieved it quickly enough (Maczulak, 2007).

Urban legends sometimes involved numbers. For example, persons alleged that the number 23 had an extraordinary significance. After noting that Shakespeare was born on April 23, they pointed out that he then died fifty-two years later on April 23. They found numerous other historical incidents that corroborated this number's unusual importance.

Proponents of the number 23 myth noted that Darwin published the *Origin of Species* in 1859; they added these numbers to reveal that *1 + 8 + 5 + 9 = 23*. The atomic bomb was dropped on Hiroshima at 8:15; these numbers can be added to reveal that *8 + 15 = 23*. The 9/11/2001 attack on New York City contained numbers that also added up to 23: *9 + 11 + 2 + 0 + 0 + 1 = 23*. Enthusiasts discerned scores of examples that demonstrated the presence of this number in the arts, sciences, humanities, business, government, and popular culture ("Number 23 Frequency Enigma," 2009).

Some urban legends resembled morality tales. One of these recounted the ordeals of a husband on a business trip. The husband met an attractive female, returned with her to a hotel room, drank a cocktail, became dazed, and passed out.

When he later recovered, the husband realized that he was alone in a bathtub full of ice. He also realized that his cell phone and a note had been placed next to the tub. Still groggy, the husband read the note. It informed him that his kidney had been removed. It emphasized that his only hope for survival was to call the number on the note, which would summon the paramedics. The husband grabbed the phone and hurriedly followed the advice.

When the paramedics arrived, they confirmed that the information on the note was correct—the husband's kidney had been removed. They also confirmed that he was the latest victim in a dastardly string of crimes. They explained that thieves had been using the identical ruse to sedate persons, operate on them, remove organs, and then ship the organs overseas (Emery, 2008).

HISTORICAL CONTRARIANS

Some persons not only believed urban legends but tried to persuade other persons to profess them. They exhibited this pattern of behavior on numerous occasions.

Slavery

Americans suffered after the Civil War. Although both Northerners and Southerners had to deal with problems, one group faced problems that were less severe. The Northerners, who had waged war primarily in the Southern states, had been able to sustain their communities, their way of life, and their economy. In fact, many Northern industrialists prospered because of the war.

Southern white citizens were in different positions. They had to rebuild homes, civic buildings, factories, railways, roads, bridges, and harbors. They had to regenerate farming, commerce, and industry. They had to care for hundreds of thousands of maimed soldiers. They had to provide civic, medical, and educational services to white citizens; they also had to provide them for the first time to four million African American citizens (Gibson & Jung, 2002; Horton & Horton, 2005).

Before the Civil War, Southerners had relied on exploitation to sustain an agriculture-based economy. Although they had limited success, they attributed that success to slavery (Berlin, 2003). After the war, they created a social and economic order that was reminiscent of that during the slavery era; they segregated non-African American citizens from their African American peers.

Rationalizing Early Racial Discrimination

Some of the early slaveholders attempted to profess commitments to slavery and humanitarianism. However, they had difficulty reconciling these two sets of beliefs (Levy, 2005; Wiencek, 2003). Some of their post-bellum descendents experienced the same discomfort.

Antebellum Southerners used an intellectual sleight of hand to ease their moral and intellectual consternation. Even though they admitted that their

African American slaves lived in captivity, they convinced themselves that they enjoyed their lives. They speculated that terrible fates would have befallen them had they been released. They insisted that the slaves as well as the masters had recognized the benefits of this codependent relationship (Dudley, 1992; Kennedy, 2003).

Rationalizing Later Racial Discrimination

The post-bellum white Southerners had created a society in which they controlled government, business, and education. They discerned dramatic disparities between their lives and those of African American citizens. Like their ancestors, they suffered intellectual and moral anguish. Like them, they wished to ease their anguish.

The post-bellum white Southerners reasoned that social, economic, and political disparities were inevitable because of the different aptitudes and temperaments of the two races. They insisted that African American citizens continued to relish a society where their intellectually and morally superior white peers were in charge.

White Southerners used rhetorical legerdemain similar to that which their ancestors had employed. For this reason, they hoped that they would be able to revise the prevailing attitudes about those ancestors.

White Southerners argued that the slaveholders had treated African Americans humanely. Nonetheless, they had a difficult time explaining why supposedly content slaves had risked their lives to escape from their masters and organize revolts against them (Blight, 2004; Greenberg, 2003; Osagie, 2000).

Contrarian historians continued to have difficulties when they tried to explain post-Civil War incidents. They could not explain why white citizens condoned mob lynchings, brutal assaults, and the terrorist acts of the Ku Klux Klan (Brundage, 1997; Chalmers, 2003; Dray, 2002; MacLean, 1994; Vandiver, 2006). They could not explain why twentieth-century African Americans led the Civil Rights Movement (Romano & Raiford, 2006).

The Holocaust

Most Americans publicly decried racism. They resolved that they would battle it ruthlessly, especially when it affected children. In spite of their public statements and bold resolutions, they had difficulty recognizing racism in their own communities (Feagin & McKinney, 2003; Fredrickson, 2002; Rattansi, 2007; Van Ausdale & Feagin, 2001).

Because Americans had difficulty detecting the racist acts for which they were responsible, they allowed them to germinate, grow, blossom, and spread (Constantine & Sue, 2006). They reacted similarly to acts of religious discrimination.

Rationalizing Early Religious Discrimination

Even though most Americans publicly decried religious discrimination and vowed that they would combat it, they treated many groups offensively. For example, they treated Jews with overt and covert disdain. They discriminated overtly when they enacted anti-Semitic restrictions in workplaces, neighborhoods, and schools; they discriminated covertly when they suppressed the genuine rationale for those restrictions (Laqueur, 2006; Rosenbaum, 2004).

Jews protested against anti-Semitism. They reminded persons of the historical incidents in which anti-Semitism had led to violence. They also reminded them of contemporary incidents. Prior to World War II, they documented the violence directed at Jews in Europe and the Soviet Union. They entreated their fellow Americans to intervene (Gross, 2006; James, 2001; Weiss, 2003).

Even though skeptics were presented with incontrovertible evidence before and during the war, they refused to acknowledge the Holocaust. When they eventually viewed the postwar newsreels of victims in concentration camps, all but the most hardened anti-Semites conceded that six million Jews had been imprisoned, tortured, and murdered.

Members of the American public commiserated with the Jews who had perished in the Holocaust; they also sympathized with those who had survived. They wanted to create a community where displaced Jews could settle. They supported the creation of a distinctively Jewish nation: Israel.

Americans were moved emotionally and intellectually by the Holocaust; they adopted new attitudes towards Jews who lived abroad and in the United States. Although they did not suppress anti-Semitism, they reduced it to a level that was lower than it was before the war (Giordano, 2009).

Americans took actions to decrease anti-Semitism in the schools. Some of them concentrated on textbooks. For example, they removed the anti-Semitic references in them. Some of them replaced offensive passages with material about the contributions of Jews to the arts, sciences, education, and government. Others made sure that the schoolbooks contained information about the horrors of the Holocaust (Giordano, 2003, 2009).

Rationalizing Later Religious Discrimination

Immediately after World War II, anti-Semites realized that most Americans were horrified by the Holocaust; they had a difficult time finding persons to join their ranks. Nonetheless, they predicted that these attitudes would shift. They were correct. Attitudes shifted in response to the Israeli-Arab conflicts, terrorism in the Middle East, terrorism around the globe, and domestic situations in the United States (Chesler, 2003; Falk, 2008).

Post-World War II anti-Semites decided to borrow a strategy from the segregationists. Just as the segregationists raised questions about the genuine nature of slavery, the anti-Semites raised questions about the Holocaust.

In the case of slavery, the segregationists could not challenge the reality of slavery. After all, four million men, women, and children had been emancipated at the end of the Civil War. Instead of challenging whether slavery had existed, they challenged whether African Americans had viewed it as an oppressive and cruel practice; they claimed that they joyfully had participated in it.

Like the American segregationists, anti-Semites wished to revise the prevailing views about extraordinarily inhumane events (Thomas, 1993). Nonetheless, they could not employ the rhetoric of the segregationists. For reasons that were self-evident, they could not contend that the Holocaust was an event in which victims participated joyfully. Therefore, they employed the only other available strategy: they denied the reality of the Holocaust.

Some Holocaust deniers refused to admit that six million Jews were arrested, abused, and exterminated. Others, who admitted that Jews were arrested, challenged the assertions that they were subjected to atrocities. Still others, who conceded that atrocities had occurred, insisted that a relatively insignificant number of Jews had perished (B'nai B'rith, 1993; Lipstadt, 1993; Stern, 1993).

The persons who denied the Holocaust had diverse political and ideological motives (Harrison, 2006; Shermer & Grobman, 2000; Zimmerman, 2000). Nonetheless, all of them shared several characteristics: they made brash assertions, ignored contradictory evidence, and relished the damage that they inflicted.

EDUCATIONAL CONTRARIANS

Historical contrarians rejected prevailing explanations for events; they devised their own accounts. They clung to their accounts when they lacked supportive evidence; they clung to them when they encountered conflicting evidence. Educational contrarians behaved in similar fashions.

Special Education

Many nineteenth-century Americans were frightened of persons with disabilities. Some of them wished to confine them in asylums, prisons, or residential hospitals. Others wanted to find a less expensive way to restrict them.

The parents of children with disabilities did not share the prevalent fears. They did not want to send their children to distant asylums, where they were sure they would be mistreated. They wanted their children to receive humane care in their own communities. They attracted the support of physicians, educators, social reformers, and religious leaders.

Parents and their allies demanded humane care for children with disabilities. They even had a plan of action. They urged American educators to follow the lead of the Europeans, who were providing daycare and instruction at local schools.

Early School Administrators

In response to pressure from their constituents, American educators opened the public schools to children with disabilities. The educators in Massachusetts, Rhode Island, New York, and several other states led the way during the late 1800s and early 1900s. Educators in the other areas followed their example.

After they admitted children with disabilities, school administrators had to deal with practical problems. They had to train teachers, locate equipment, designate facilities, create learning materials, and establish curricula. They had difficulty because their funds were limited. However, they also had difficulty because they lacked sound advice. Although they turned to scholars for help, they were discouraged by their endless squabbling (Giordano, 2007).

School administrators had difficulty assigning students to special education. Unable to get sound advice from scholars, they relied on their own intuitions. They did assign many children with genuine disabilities to special education programs. However, they also assigned children who had behavioral problems, came from impoverished families, represented racial minority groups, had limited skills in English, or merely were eccentric (Giordano, 2007).

Contrarians

For decades, educators struggled when they had to make decisions about the children that would participate in special education. Even when they tried to make these decisions fairly and objectively, they upset many parents. The disgruntled parents eventually asked federal legislators to help them.

Members of Congress enacted an unprecedented piece of legislation during the 1970s. They required school administrators to employ common procedures to identify special education students. They even provided funds to help them make the transition to the new procedures (Education for All Handicapped Children Act, 1975).

Although school administrators were required to follow guidelines about the children that would participate in special education, they still exercised great discretion. Therefore, the members of Congress took an addition step: they required the United States Office of Education to monitor whether the school administrators were complying with the new regulations.

The federal educational authorities wished to ensure that school administrators followed the details and the spirit of regulations. They began by assembling profiles of the students in local programs. They assumed that these profiles would reflect those of the students in other programs. For example, if thirty percent of the students in special education were minority students, they assumed that thirty percent of other students would be minority students.

Some school administrators challenged the assumptions about the profiles of special education students. They argued that economic and community factors made their profiles unpredictable. They suggested that these factors explained why high numbers of minority children were being assigned to special education (Giordano, 2007).

After they reviewed data, federal bureaucrats were disturbed by the disproportionate number of African American students in special education. Nonetheless, they proceeded cautiously. Aware that the irregularities might be temporary, they did not charge discrimination.

Federal bureaucrats collected data for decades. At the end of that period, they concluded that the overrepresentation of minority children was an enduring and pervasive trend in special education (Markowitz, 1996; Markowitz, Garcia, & Eichelberger, 1997). Furthermore, they attributed the overrepresentation to discrimination. Other analysts agreed with them (Grossman, 1998; Losen & Orfield, 2002). They advised school personnel to correct the problem (Burnette, 1998; Kalyanpur & Harry, 1999; Shea & Bauer, 1994).

Some school administrators disregarded the accusations of racial discrimination. They insisted that a disproportionately high representation of minority special education students was appropriate and possibly inevitable.

Standardized Testing

Standardized testing has been controversial for decades. Members of the public were upset about it during World War I. They were disturbed because many recruits had scored poorly on the military's standardized intelligence tests. They became even more disturbed after conservative politicians and journalists warned that the low scores revealed a national crisis.

Early Opponents

Walter Lippmann was an influential World War I journalist who questioned whether the scores on standardized tests demonstrated genuine problems. He berated the alarmists for using standardized tests as political tools. He attracted a group of ardent sympathizers.

Once World War I was over, the opponents of standardized tests continued to repeat Lippmann's arguments. They also came up with additional arguments. They claimed that the tests relied on contrived tasks, employed inappropriate statistical concepts, and exhibited social biases (Giordano, 2005).

Although testing opponents were evident throughout the twentieth century, they generated great publicity during the 1970s. Ralph Nader and a group of consumer advocates remonstrated against the Educational Testing Service, a nonprofit agency that published high-profile exams.

Nader and his colleagues berated the Educational Testing Service for excessive secrecy. They claimed that it refused to disclose data that consumers needed to determine whether tests were fair. They especially were concerned about the tests that university applicants completed. They claimed that the Educational Testing Service had jeopardized applicants' educations and careers with these tests.

Although members of the public initially were curious about the anti-testing protests, they eventually lost interest. Most members of the public—as well as most school administrators, employers, and politicians—continued to value standardized tests. They explained that they valued them because they provided critical information.

Critics realized that they had to do more than attack standardized tests; they had to provide an alternative way to gather critical information. They hoped that informally administered tests would solve this problem. They counseled school teachers to observe students, compile samples of their work, and maintain detailed records of their achievements. They predicted that this comprehensive type of record keeping would be as useful as standardized testing and that it would not have its disadvantages (Giordano, 2005).

Politicians and businesspersons were wary of informally administered tests. They anticipated that these tests would be administered and interpreted differently from school to school; they worried that they might vary significantly from teacher to teacher in the same school.

Many educators also were concerned about informal assessment procedures. They worried that they might be cumbersome and time-consuming.
They also worried that they might be invalid. Parents and educational stakeholders shared their concerns.

Contrarians

The proponents of informal tests realized that they would have a hard time
demonstrating that their assessment procedures were efficient, reliable, and
valid. Therefore, they addressed these challenges obliquely by claiming that
standardized tests had as many problems as informal tests.

Although the proponents of informal tests attacked all types of standardized tests, they concentrated on intelligence tests. They complained that
these tests measured only verbal, mathematical, and logical abilities. They
explained that they failed to measure another critical trait: emotional ability.

The proponents of informal tests argued that emotional ability enabled persons to succeed in social situations. They asserted that it was just as important
as verbal, mathematical, or logical ability; they insisted that it was a valid
type of intelligence (Andrews, 2004; Ciarrochi, Forgas, & Mayer, 2006;
Goleman, 1995; Matthews, Zeidner, & Roberts, 2007; Wilding, 2007).

Enthusiasts were sure that persons with high measures of emotional intelligence could make contributions that were as valuable as those of persons with
highs scores on traditional intelligence tests. They provided advice to teachers about how to assess and develop emotional intelligence (Bar-On, Maree,
& Elias, 2007; Lewkowicz, 2007). They even advised businesspersons about
emotional intelligence in the workplace (Cherniss & Goleman, 2001).

When persons completed traditional intelligence tests, half of them scored
below the median. Understandably, they were disappointed. However, those
who professed belief in emotional intelligence could request another evalua-
tion—one that assessed emotional intelligence. Some of them viewed emotional
intelligence as a way to raise their stature; others viewed it as a way to reduce the
stature of persons who had scored high on traditional intelligence tests.

Although some critics denigrated standardized tests for failing to measure
emotional intelligence, others amplified this criticism. They claimed that
standardized tests failed to measure multiple types of intelligence. Howard
Gardner was an influential educator who postulated that intelligence could
be verbal, logical, mathematical, emotional, spatial, kinesthetic, musical, or
intrapersonal (Gardner, 1983, 1999).

Persons who were enthusiastic about multiple types of intelligence demonstrated traits that were similar to those that the enthusiasts for emotional
intelligence demonstrated. They expounded on educational implications, elaborated vocational applications, and promoted informal assessment techniques

(Armstrong, 2003; Gardner, 2007; Lazear, 1994). They shared one more trait with the proponents of emotional intelligence: they were barraged with criticism (Murphy, 2006; Schaler, 2006).

EXAMINING CONTRARIAN ADVICE

Contrarians made contentions about popular culture, politics, history, and education. They rejected prevailing explanations and endorsed uncorroborated accounts. They persisted in the face of contradictory evidence.

Activity 8.1

You may wish to examine controversial contentions. You could analyze contentions about educational and non-educational topics. You could use Table 8.1.

Table 8.1 lists contentions related to five topics: urban legends, American slaves, Holocaust victims, minority students in special education, and multiple types of intelligence.

Use symbols to complete Table 8.1. Use the symbol – if corroborating evidence was not available. Use the symbol –/+ if corroborating evidence might have been available and the symbol + if it was available. You also can use these symbols to indicate the availability of contradictory evidence. Explain your selections.

To complete the table, you could rely on the information in this chapter, the books that are cited in it, additional books, or your personal experiences.

Activity 8.2

You might wish to examine controversial contentions from another perspective. For example, you might wish to hypothesize about the ways in which groups reacted to contentions about educational and non-educational topics. You could use Table 8.2.

Table 8.2 identifies controversial contentions related to five topics: urban legends, American slaves, Holocaust victims, minority students in special education, and multiple types of intelligence. It also identifies two groups: educators and members of the general public.

Hypothesize about the ways in which educators and members of the general public reacted to the contentions in the table. Use the symbol – if the members of the group were not supportive. Use the symbol –/+ if they exhibited a mixed reaction and the symbol + if they were supportive. As a final step, explain the basis for the symbols that you selected.

Table 8.1.   Controversial Contentions

Contention	Evidence*		Explanation
	Corroborating	Contradicting	
Urban Legends			
American Slaves			
Holocaust Victims			
Minority Students in Special Education			
Multiple Types of Intelligence			

* (–) Not Available
(–/+) Possibly Available
(+) Available

Table 8.2.   Reactions to Controversial Contentions

Contention	Group*		Explanation
	Educators	General Public	
Urban Legends			
American Slaves			
Holocaust Victims			
Minority Students in Special Education			
Multiple Types of Intelligence			

* (–) Not Supportive
(–/+) Mixed Reaction
(+) Supportive

Activity 8.3

You might wish to consider controversial contentions from still another perspective. You could hypothesize about the ways in which groups reacted to educational contentions. You could use Table 8.3.

Table 8.3 lists two groups: educators and the general public. It also lists several controversial contentions. It lists contentions related to minority students in special education and multiple types of intelligence. It gives you the chance to identify one more contention. You could identify the third contention by yourself, with another reader, or with a small group of readers.

Indicate the ways in which educators and the general public reacted to the contentions in this table. Use the symbols in the legend. Finally, explain your selections.

Table 8.3. Reactions to Controversial Educational Contentions

| Contention | Group* | | Explanation |
	Educators	General Public	
Minority Students in Special Education			
Multiple Types of Intelligence			
Other:			

* (–) Not Supportive
(–/+) Mixed Reaction
(+) Supportive

SUMMARY

Contrarians challenged the prevailing views about numerous incidents and issues. They sometimes challenged the prevailing views about education.

Chapter 9

Should Politicians
Manage Classrooms?

[The government should support] free education for all children in public schools [and the] abolition of children's factory labor.

—Karl Marx & Friedrich Engels, 1848

When citizens asked politicians to help with the problems in the schools, they had complex motives. When the politicians considered how to respond, they also had complex motives.

COMMUNIST ISSUES

In the ancient world, scholars gave politicians advice about education. They attempted to make that advice as influential as possible. During subsequent eras, they still were concerned about this issue. For example, the philosopher John Locke wondered how to give educational advice that was substantive and influential. He decided to follow the example of many other scholars when he presented it within an esoteric treatise (Locke, 1947).

Locke's eighteenth-century recommendations did not have the impact that he had hoped they would. A century and a half later, two scholars again tried to ensure that their educational recommendations were influential. They came up with a novel idea: they incorporated their advice into a political document. The scholars were Karl Marx and Friedrich Engels.

When they wrote the *Communist Manifesto,* Marx and Engels decided to address laborers rather than politicians. They counseled them that they had been mistreated by industrialists. They adjured them to rebel, join labor unions, profess communism, and establish a society in which all wealth would be distributed equitably (Marx & Engels, 1848).

Although they assured readers that an Elysian society was approaching, Marx and Engels told them how to manage affairs during the transition. They instructed them to abolish private property, impose progressive income taxes, and centralize banking. They also urged them to remove children from workplaces and send them to public schools.

Some nineteenth-century scholars were excited about the recommendations of Marx and Engels. Others remained excited long afterward (Apple, 2001; Freire, 1970, 1985; Moe, 2001; Westheimer, 2007). However, many persons were alarmed.

Political conservatives were alarmed by the goals and the strategies of the communists. Nonetheless, they were intrigued by the way in which they had made education into a political tool. They wondered whether they would be able to use it in the same fashion (Bloom, 1987; Horowitz, 2006, 2007).

WARTIME ISSUES

Prior to World War I, American politicians searched for an educational issue with which to attract attention, money, and constituents. They judged that universal, mandatory schooling might be the perfect issue.

Some politicians endorsed universal schooling because they wanted to remove children from dangerous workplaces and give them chances to prosper. Others supported it for a different reason: they wanted to win the support of union members. The union members were upset that they had to compete with children for jobs. They complained that the children had advantages because they accepted hazardous jobs, worked for low wages, and responded readily to intimidation.

Not all politicians supported universal schooling. Some of them opposed it because they believed it was unconstitutional. Others opposed it because they hoped to win the approval of the businesspersons who depended on child laborers. The politicians detected many other opportunities to gain their approval. They saw chances to help them sell textbooks, tests, classroom technology, vocational machinery, school transportation, playground equipment, clerical products, buildings, maintenance products, classroom furniture, and innumerable other items (Giordano, 2003, 2009).

Early twentieth-century politicians had been involved with education. They hoped to use it to increase their influence. In spite of these early experiences, they became much more involved with it after the United States entered World War I.

World War I

Conservative and liberal politicians had sparred over education throughout the late 1800s and the early 1900s; they continued to trade jabs during World War I. Even though many of the conservatives were members of the Republican Party, they supported a Democratic president, Woodrow Wilson.

Wilson, who narrowly won a second term in 1916, had run on a promise to keep the United States at peace. However, he changed his mind after the election. He explained that he switched positions after he had realized that a "war to end all war" was the best way to promote peace.

Wilson ignored his pro-neutrality constituents; he adjured every man and woman to participate in the war effort. Directing a good deal of rhetoric at the schools, he encouraged the school administrators and teachers to get involved. He even urged students to take part. He encouraged young children to gather scrap materials and invest in government savings programs; he implored adolescents to prepare for the military services or wartime factories (Giordano, 2004).

Conservative politicians were delighted with Wilson's wartime school programs. However, they hoped that the war would give them the chance to address some of their other educational worries. For example, they worried that children were less patriotic than their parents and grandparents. They also worried about immigrant children, whom they believed were unwilling to abandon non-English languages, distinctive ethnic practices, and loyalties to former countries.

The conservatives claimed that schools caused problems by failing to nurture American nationalism; they alleged that they actually undermined nationalism in some communities. They were upset that German-American communities allowed public-school teachers to conduct classes in German and use textbooks that had been published in Germany. They called for laws to curtail these practices. Some of them wanted to go further and exclude German from the foreign-language curricula of all high schools (Giordano, 2004).

Conservative politicians ardently supported President Wilson's domestic wartime initiatives. They also supported another initiative—the army's new assessment system. After war had been declared, military leaders had searched for a way to assess and classify the millions of young men that were being assigned to them. They asked psychologists to help them measure the soldiers' intelligence, suitability for the armed services, and career aptitudes. The psychologists responded with standardized tests (Giordano, 2005).

Members of the public were fascinated by the originality and the scope of the army's assessment project. However, they were disconcerted by its results. In fact, they were alarmed after they learned that hundreds of thousands of soldiers had earned test scores no higher than those of children.

Conservative politicians expressed shock at the many servicemen who were scoring low on intelligence tests. They claimed that their scores revealed a national problem. Although they blamed the schools for creating this problem, they praised tests for uncovering it.

Post-World War I

Conservatives made numerous changes in the schools during World War I. They expanded the use of textbooks with flattering descriptions of America's economy, foreign policy, institutions, government, and heritage. They implemented standardized tests, industrial education, patriotic practices, projects to train males for the armed services, and advanced programs in science, mathematics, technology, and physical education.

Once World War I was over, the conservatives intended to preserve their gains; they wanted to retain the scholastic practices that enhanced national security. However, they were opposed by the postwar liberals.

The liberals claimed that the military-like practices resembled those that the Germans had used to inculcate chauvinism. They characterized standardized tests as confusing, unreliable, and invalid. They blamed the scholastic emphases on science, mathematics, technology, physical education, and industrial education for pushing music, drama, and art out of the curriculum (Giordano, 2004).

During World War I, the conservatives had supported Woodrow Wilson. During the era between the world wars, they rallied around another political liberal, President Franklin Roosevelt. Like Wilson, Roosevelt vowed to keep the United States out of war. However, he shipped war materiel to the Allied forces, modernized America's armed services, established conscription, and implemented school-based propaganda programs.

Roosevelt repeatedly averred that he had accelerated national defense programs to discourage aggression. Nonetheless, many of his liberal constituents questioned his sincerity.

World War II

When President Roosevelt commenced his wartime school initiatives, he patterned them after those of Wilson. However, he timed them differently. While Wilson had introduced programs *after* the United States had entered a conflict, Roosevelt introduced them *before* the country had declared war.

The students in the wartime programs performed calisthenic exercises, wore uniforms, learned military procedures, marched in formation, and drilled with rifles. They gathered money, salvaged recyclable materials, and raised crops for the war. Some of them learned vocations and became part-time workers in the defense factories (Giordano, 2004).

Political conservatives supported Roosevelt's school initiatives. They also supported some of his other wartime domestic policies. They supported the creation of boards to censor wartime news and entertainment; they supported the arrest and imprisonment of Japanese Americans.

The Fifties

Roosevelt campaigned for a fourth presidential term while the country was still at war. Although he won the election, he died at the beginning of that term. He was succeeded by Vice President Harry Truman. Truman profited politically from the positive attitudes that Americans displayed during war. However, he was a World War II leader for only several months.

Truman treasured the unified and supportive spirit that the wartime public had demonstrated. He watched that spirit subside after the war. He hoped that a military campaign in Korea and the propaganda associated with it would help him regain national approval. However, he had limited success.

After he sent troops into Korea, Truman did not detect a return of the nation's positive martial spirit. Quite the opposite, he detected resentment, frustration, and anger. He was disconcerted by the sharp barbs that journalists and rival politicians hurled at him; he was even more upset by the displeasure of the public. He realized that his constituents were ready for a new president.

Voters selected Dwight Eisenhower to succeed Truman. They were reassured by Eisenhower's military stature, political competence, and serene demeanor. Nonetheless, they were unsettled by international events, such as the Soviet Union's launch of the *Sputnik* satellite.

Conservative politicians fanned the embers of public unrest into flames of apprehension. They warned that the United States was lagging behind the Soviet Union. They claimed that schools in the United States could not train scientists who were as qualified as the Soviet scientists. They concluded that inferior schools imperiled America's security. As they looked for groups to blame, they focused on teachers and school administrators (Giordano, 2004).

The Vietnam War

During the early years of the Cold War, Truman hoped that educational propaganda would advance his foreign policies. His successors also tried to use it in this fashion. However, they concentrated on college propaganda.

Several presidents waged a controversial war in Vietnam. President Kennedy, who was assassinated during the first phase of that war, did not have to deal with dissidents. Presidents Johnson and Nixon, who expanded the scope of the war, had to confront protesters throughout society. They paid particular attention to the dissidents on college campuses.

Johnson and Nixon were upset with the college students who convened large, well organized, vocal, and sustained protests. They also were upset with journalists, who they viewed as compatriots of the students. They accused the journalists of sympathizing with students, misrepresenting the events on campuses, and creating public consternation (Perlstein, 2008).

Johnson initially attempted to change the attitudes of college students with propaganda. Aware that citizens in earlier generations had supported wars to halt international aggression, he depicted the current conflict as a similar type of war. He declared that the United States was fighting to prevent aggressors from taking control of southeast Asia and the world.

Johnson was upset when college students derided his logic; he was furious when they escalated their protests. He tried to subdue them with police and military force. He became depressed after his actions had the opposite effects: they caused the number of antiwar protesters to grow and his popularity to diminish.

Johnson was succeeded by Richard Nixon. Nixon replicated the tactics that Johnson had employed with the college dissidents. However, he had even less luck with them. He eventually withdrew American troops from Vietnam.

Late Twentieth Century

Political analysts predicted that the presidents who followed Johnson and Nixon would pursue foreign policy less aggressively. Presidents Gerald Ford and Jimmy Carter confirmed those predictions (Freedman, 2008). However, each of these men served for a relatively short period. They were succeeded by Ronald Reagan, a president who served for eight years and who had a different temperament from his two predecessors.

Early in Reagan's first term, the United States Department of Education published a report about the students in the American schools. It used the report's title, *A Nation at Risk,* to foreshadow the central message within it (National Commission on Excellence in Education, 1983). Borrowing rhetoric from the early conservatives, the report's authors asserted that students in the United States were unable to compete with those in other countries; they warned that they endangered America's economy and national security.

A Nation at Risk created a sensation. The bureaucrats at the national Department of Education were thrilled; they kept records of the newspapers and magazines in which the report was discussed (Giordano, 2005). Even educators who disagreed with the report conceded that it caused a commotion; in fact, they acknowledged that it produced a stir for decades (Gordon, 2003; Hayes, 2004; Lund, 1993; Peterson & Chubb, 2003).

DOMESTIC ISSUES

Woodrow Wilson and Franklin Roosevelt served as presidents during eras of national unity. They used education to strengthen that unity and advance international initiatives. Later presidents were less successful when they used education to enhance foreign policy. However, they used it for other purposes. For example, they used it to reward constituents.

President Jimmy Carter was elected with the support of unionized educators. He was urged by Joseph Califano, his Secretary of Health, Education, and Welfare, to repay them. He acceded to the secretary's advice (Califano, 1981, 2004).

Carter took steps to win the approbation of educators. He established a national department of education and a cabinet-level secretary to manage it. He provided funding for bilingual education, protection for minority children, and advocacy for children with disabilities (Mathews, 1988).

Carter hoped that the favors that he had done for his constituents would secure another term for him. However, he lost the 1982 presidential election to Ronald Reagan. Having replaced Carter, Reagan changed the national educational priorities. He revealed his distinctive priorities when he pledged to eliminate the Department of Education.

Although he was unable to abolish the Department of Education, Reagan did neutralize some of Carter's other key initiatives. He substantially reduced the funding for the programs that were directed at bilingual learners and impoverished children. He then encouraged communities to substitute state or private funds for the money that he had withdrawn (Berube, 1991; "President Reagan's 1984 Education," 1983).

President Reagan endorsed the educational initiatives that conservative constituents supported. For example, he endorsed programs to help academically talented students and bolster national defense. Even though he assigned high priority to these programs, he was reluctant to spend federal money on them (David, 1982; Reinhold, 1982).

The fiscally conservative Reagan looked for an inexpensive opportunity to reward conservative constituents. He conjectured that school prayer could be the ideal opportunity. School prayer, which once had been ubiquitous in public education, had been virtually eliminated by court actions (DelFattore,

2004; Gaddy, Hall, & Marzano, 1996; Greenawalt, 2005; Kunzman, 2006; Thomas, 2007). Reagan opposed these court actions and called for a constitutional amendment to block additional judiciary interventions ("Reagan Backs Bill," 1982).

President Reagan reacted predictably to educational issues. Other conservatives followed the same pattern. Nonetheless, they sometimes surprised their constituents. They surprised them when they partnered with liberal colleagues to reform special education during the 1970s; they surprised them again when they persuaded Gerald Ford, a Republican president, to sign the reform legislation (Davies, 2007; Giordano, 2007).

The conservatives surprised their constituents on other occasions. During the 1980s, they joined liberals to prevent Reagan from weakening the legal rights of students with disabilities (Hunter, 1982). During the 1990s, they supported the American Disabilities Act, which defined the rights of persons with disabilities in public facilities. They then advised George H. W. Bush, the Republican president, to sign that act (Giordano, 2007).

Like the conservatives, liberals sometimes took unexpected educational stances. President Clinton startled unionized educational workers when he announced that he would rely on standardized tests to monitor school progress (Giordano, 2005). Even though he disconcerted his traditional constituents, Clinton used his position on testing to form political alliances with other constituents (McAndrews, 2006).

When liberal or conservative politicians reacted unexpectedly to educational issues, they had to resist pressure from lobbyists (Benoit, 2007; Nownes, 2006). They also had to resist pressure from partisan journalists (Coulter, 2006; Moore, 2003; O'Reilly, 2001) and organized groups of voters (Adams, 2007; Blackwell, 2006; Bootel, 1995, 1999; Cooper, Cibulka, & Fusarelli, 2008; Fiedler & Clark, 2008; National School Boards Association, 1995).

Politicians who aspired to be president took positions to expand their voter appeal. They revealed their educational positions when they engaged in interviews, delivered speeches, and wrote books (e.g., Clinton, 2003; Goldwater, 1960; Gore, 2007; Kennedy, 1964; Obama, 2006). Former presidents, who wished to preserve their influence, used these opportunities to proclaim their educational positions (Carter, 2005; Clinton, 2004; Nixon, 1978; Reagan, 1990).

Pragmatic politicians hired writers, marketers, and consultants to help them mold statements about education. Some of them, such as John Kennedy and Barry Goldwater, tried to conceal the degree to which they depended on consultants (Perlstein, 2001; Schlesinger, 2008); others, such as Ronald Reagan, Newt Gingrich, and John McCain, openly acknowledged their dependence (Gingrich, Haley, & Tyler, 2008; Kirkpatrick, 2008; McCain & Salter, 2007; Reagan & Brinkley, 2007).

Science Education

When politicians crafted stances on education, they had both ulterior and altruistic motives. Some of them revealed their ulterior motives in the ways that they reacted to incidents involving education and science. The most famous incident occurred during the 1920s in a rural Southern community.

Early Disagreements

After he discussed biological evolution with his high school students, John Scopes was accused of violating a Tennessee law. Scopes, who acknowledged the discussion, chose to go to court rather than pay a fine. The American Civil Liberties Union arranged for Clarence Darrow, a preeminent defense attorney, to represent him.

Scopes, Darrow, and the American Civil Liberties Union had hoped that journalists would bring this trial to the attention of a wide audience. The journalists complied. They wrote with gusto about the trial, prohibitions against scientific information in the schools, and the prevailing social attitudes about biological evolution.

After the trial ended, the citizens who opposed evolution were gratified. The local court convicted Scopes. The Tennessee Supreme Court upheld the lower court's verdict and affirmed the constitutionality of the anti-evolution law under which Scopes had been charged.

Citizens who supported evolution also were gratified. They were pleased that the trial had generated national and international publicity for their point of view. Nonetheless, they were not completely satisfied. They continued to insist that evolution be taught in the public schools. They gained increasing support from the courts (Beckwith, 2003; Geisler, 2007; Giordano, 2003; Larson, 2003).

Later Disagreements

During the 1920s, the creationists occupied the strategic high ground. From this camp, they were able to persuade state legislators to introduce thirty-seven anti-evolution teaching bills. However, the courts forced them to abandon their advantageous position (Giordano, 2003).

Even though they began to lose most legal skirmishes, the creationists were not ready to surrender. They were convinced that "intelligent design" and "scientific creationism" were worthwhile explanations for the beginning of life and biological change. They argued that these explanations constituted plausible, scientific theories; they pleaded with school administrators to incorporate them into the science curricula (Bergman & Wirth, 2008; Morris, 1985; Rana, 2008; Sharp & Bergman, 2008).

Like the creationists, the evolution advocates were ardent. They displayed their passion in numerous ways, including the titles that they selected for their books. They chose deliberately confrontational titles such as *Evolution and the Myth of Creationism, Triumph of Evolution, Creationism's Trojan Horse,* and *Why Intelligent Design Fails* (Berra, 1990; Eldredge, 2000; Forrest & Gross, 2004; Young & Edis, 2004).

Even though the creationists were able to maintain the backing of state legislatures, they could not maintain that of the courts. As their fortunes changed, they realized that creationism was being removed from science curricula and that evolution was being firmly embedded within them. They were worried that creationist teachers would be prosecuted for violating constitutional restrictions on religion in the schools. They once again asked state legislators to intervene.

The creationists asked legislators to protect teachers who instructed students about creationism. They were pleased when Florida legislators introduced protective bills in 2008; they especially were pleased because the Floridians coordinated their efforts with legislators in Alabama, Arkansas, Georgia, Michigan, Missouri, Oklahoma, and South Carolina. They urged the members of this legislative alliance to pass pro-creation laws that were similar to the laws that Louisiana already had enacted (Boyd, 2009; Sorgel, 2009).

Retrospective on Science in the Schools

The public's beliefs about creationism and evolution were stable at the end of the twentieth century. The number of persons declaring a belief in creationism and the number professing a belief in evolution had remained the same throughout the 1980s. The two groups continued to be comparably sized for a multi-decade period (Newport, 2008).

Even though the attitudes of the general public were split evenly, the attitudes of Republicans and Democrats differed. Sixty percent of Republicans were sure that a divine being had created humans, that he had created them ten thousand years ago, and that he had created them in their present form. Only thirty-eight percent of Democrats agreed with these contentions (Newport, 2008).

In the disputes about the world's origin, one faction attracted scientists while the other attracted fundamentalist Christians. Because Democratic politicians vocally supported evolution, they attracted the scientists; because Republican politicians loudly supported creationism, they attracted fundamentalist Christians.

Once the Republicans had attracted fundamentalist Christian voters, they wished to keep them in their party. During his eight-year tenure, President George W. Bush took numerous steps to retain their allegiance. He highlighted the ways in which religion influenced his party's foreign policies (Slater, 2007), government-funded research priorities (Babington, 2006; Rozell & Whitney, 2007), and social programs (Daly, 2006; Goodstein, 2001; Kuo, 2006; Owens, 2007).

In spite of some highly publicized stances against science, the Republicans historically were committed to science in the schools. In fact, they frequently took the lead. During World War I, they were worried that the educators in enemy countries were doing a better job than those in the United States; they adjured American educators to offer more science courses, enrich science curricula, and prepare a greater number of students for scientific careers. They also campaigned to incorporate a scientific assessment system into the schools. They continued to support these initiatives during the subsequent era, World War II, and the Cold War.

Many Democrats were upset when the Republicans championed science education. They accused them of using it as a political ploy with which to advance non-educational initiatives. However, the Republicans made the same accusation when the Democrats depicted education as an antidote for economic problems.

Education as Economic Stimulus

Democrats and Republicans had used fear as a political tool. The early twentieth-century Republicans had used fear to make changes in the schools. They continued to use it for decades. George W. Bush used fear of terrorism to make pervasive social changes. As just one example, he imposed travel measures that not only increased security but that also conveyed the rationale for his foreign policies (Brill, 2003; Mayer, 2008; Suskind, 2006).

After Bush had completed two terms, the Republicans were mired in congressional and presidential campaigns. They attempted to retain international threats as the focal point of these contests. They urged voters to keep them in power so that they could protect the nation. However, voters had changed their priorities.

Voters were more worried about economic perils than international threats. They were terrified by plunging stock markets, defaulting banks, disappearing jobs, accelerating home foreclosures, increasing bankruptcies, surging oil prices, and rising unemployment (Sieff, 2008).

The Democrats predicted that that the ways in which the two parties reacted to economic problems would decide the elections (Morales, 2008). Therefore, they accused the Republicans of creating economic problems through wrong-headed policies (Steinhauser, 2008). They adjured voters to support Barack Obama, who would enact radical economic legislation.

The Republicans eventually agreed with the Democrats about the need for radical economic actions. However, they disagreed about details. While they wanted to cut taxes, their rivals wished to create jobs and increase the funding for education. After the Democrats gained control of both legislative houses and the presidency, they had the votes to prevail.

The Democrats designed a $787 billion economic stimulus package (American Recovery and Reinvestment Act, 2009; GovTrack.us. H.R. 1—111th Congress, 2009). They originally proposed to spend over one hundred and fifty billion dollars on education; they settled for two-thirds of that amount (Dillon, 2009). Even though they had compromised, they were pleased with the final plan.

The 2009 economic stimulus package included funding for two new educational initiatives: teacher retention and the refurbishing of old school buildings (Birnbaum, 2009; Hartman, 2009). It also contained funding for established educational programs, such as those associated with the No Child Left Behind Act (United States Department of Education, 2002).

Republicans and Democrats cooperatively had enacted the No Child Left Behind Act during the first term of President George W. Bush. They made sure that this law encompassed educational benchmarks, instructional guide-lines, and assessment schedules. They also ensured that it provided funds to help the states implement it.

The Republicans controlled Congress for six of the eight years that George W. Bush was president. They were hard-pressed to find the money for home-land security, the war in Afghanistan, the war in Iraq, massive tax cuts, and severe economic problems. They provided only a portion of the money that the No Child Left Behind initiative required (Paley, 2007).

The Democrats used the 2009 stimulus bill to expand the money to sev-eral already established but only partially funded programs. In addition to funding No Child Left Behind, they funded programs that relied on school technology. They also gave financial help to educational programs for young learners, children in daycare, children with disabilities, and children living in poverty.

Critics claimed that the stimulus bill funded educational initiatives that had little relevance to the nation's economic problems. They added that it contained budgets that were too generous and spending guidelines that were too loose (Devaney, 2009; "Hold the Line," 2009; McNeil, 2009; Nagel, 2009; Samuels, 2009; "Stimulus Package and Education Funding," 2009).

EXAMINING ADVICE FROM POLITICIANS

Politicians were aware of the practical problems in the schools. However, they had to deal with partisan problems as well.

Activity 9.1

You might wish to deliberate about politicians during wartime. You could use Table 9.1.

Table 9.1 gives you opportunities to consider the ways in which conservatives and liberals reacted to school practices during World War I. It lists seven school practices: standardized testing, accelerated science education, expanded physical education, accelerated industrial education, the training of students for the armed services, the adoption of patriotic textbooks, and the exclusion of German from the foreign-language curricula of high schools.

Table 9.1. World War I School Practices

	Group*		
Practice	*Conservative*	*Liberal*	*Explanation*
Standardized Testing			
Science Education			
Physical Education			
Industrial Education			
Armed Services Training			
Patriotic Textbooks			
German Language Prohibition			

* (–) Low Support
 (–/+) Moderate Support
 (+) High Support

Use symbols to complete this table. Use the symbol + to indicate that the members of a group supported a practice. Use the symbol –/+ for moderate support and the symbol – for low support.

As a final step, provide explanations for the symbols that you selected. You can rely on the information in this chapter, the books that are cited in it, other books, or your personal experiences.

Activity 9.2

You could choose another way to analyze politicians. You could examine their reactions to recent educational practices. You could use Table 9.2.

Table 9.2 identifies educational practices to which conservatives and liberals turned their attention recently. It lists eight practices: unionization of

Table 9.2.   Recent School Practices

Practice	Group*		*Explanation*
	Conservative	*Liberal*	
Unionized Teachers			
Standardized Testing			
Testing-Based Teacher Accountability			
Bilingual Education			
Special Education			
School Prayer			
Evolution in Science Curricula			
Science Education Expansion			

* (–) Low Support
(–/+) Moderate Support
(+) High Support

teachers, standardized testing, teacher accountability that is based on standardized tests, bilingual education, special education, school prayer, evolution in science curricula, and the expansion of science education.

Use the symbols that are listed in the legend to complete this table. Explain your selections.

Activity 9.3

When deliberating about politicians and education, you might wish to consider historical and recent incidents. You could use Table 9.3.

Table 9.3. Shifting Reactions to School Practices

Era	Issue	Group* Conservative	Liberal	Explanation
World War I	Science Education			
	Evolution			
World War II	Science Education			
	Evolution			
1950s	Science Education			
	Evolution			
Late 20th Century	Science Education			
	Evolution			
Current	Science Education			
	Evolution			

* (–) Low Support
  (–/+) Moderate Support
  (+) High Support

Table 9.3 gives you chances to analyze the ways in which conservative and liberal politicians reacted to two scholastic issues: the expansion of science education programs and the inclusion of evolution within those programs.

This table gives you opportunities to identify the ways in which politicians reacted to issues during different eras. It lists five eras: World War I, World War II, the 1950s, the period at the end of the twentieth century, and the current period.

Use the symbols from the legend to complete this table. As a final step, explain your selections.

Activity 9.4

When deliberating about politicians, you might wish to consider recent instances. You could use Table 9.4.

Table 9.4 gives you chances to analyze the ways in which conservative and liberal politicians reacted to educational initiatives. It lists two federal initiatives: strengthening the mandate for standardized testing and expanding the funding for schools. It gives you chances to analyze the ways in which they reacted to these initiatives during two recent eras: the administration of George W. Bush and that of Barack Obama.

Use symbols to complete this table. You can use the symbols in the legend. As a final step, explain the basis for the symbols that you selected.

Table 9.4.   Politicians React to Current Issues

Era	Initiative	Group*		Explanation
		Conservative	Liberal	
George W. Bush	Federally Mandated Testing			
	Federally Funded Education			
Barack Obama	Federally Mandated Testing			
	Federally Funded Education			

* (–) Low Support
(–/+) Moderate Support
(+) High Support

SUMMARY

Politicians had ulterior motives when they reacted to educational issues. They revealed those motives in the ways that they responded to teacher unionization, standards-based education, standardized testing, bilingual education, special education, school prayer, school science, and the educational projects within the 2009 economic stimulus plan.

Chapter 10

Which Video Game Would Plato Prefer?

[Suppose that] human beings [have been] living in an underground den . . . from their childhood . . . [and that they] have their legs and necks chained so that they cannot move, and can only see before them . . . and behind them a fire is blazing at a distance, and between the fire and the prisoners. . . . are men . . . carrying all sorts of vessels, and statues and figures of animals. . . . and they see only their own shadows, or the shadows of one another. . . . or the objects which are being carried.

—Plato, 360 BC

Plato used metaphor-based reasoning to solve philosophical problems. Persons later used it to solve many other types of problems.

PHILOSOPHERS

Plato may have been the best-known teacher in ancient Greece. He taught the way that his mentor, Socrates, had shown him: he used the case method. In addition to teaching with this technique, he wrote with it. In his most famous book, *The Republic,* he used it to write a passage about a cave.

Plato recounted a tale about prisoners who were manacled to a rock within a cave. They were attempting to understand reality through the shadows on the wall. Plato directed his students to put themselves in the situation of the prisoners. He asked them to imagine how they would react if they were able to break free, learn about the genuine sources of the shadows, explore the cave, and discover the elaborate hoax to which they had been subjected.

Plato's students answered that they would be disconcerted. They expected to be even more upset after they left the cave and encountered a brightly lit, richly textured, and complexly colored world. They predicted that some of them would be so unnerved that they would want to go back to the cave and resume their former lives.

During the cave discussion, Plato taught his students about epistemology and metaphysics. During other discussions, he taught them about art, rhetoric, politics, ethics, mathematics, science, and education. He helped them define problems, formulate solutions, and analyze the strengths and weaknesses of solutions.

Although Plato introduced students to many solutions, he did not differentiate those that were correct or incorrect. Instead, he taught them to discern the inherent limitations of every solution. He was preparing them to deal with problems after they left him.

ARTISTS

Like philosophers, artists relied on metaphors. They used them in their creative works; they incorporated them into statues, paintings, music, poems, and novels. Some of them incorporated them into films.

In his most famous film, *The Seventh Seal,* Ingmar Bergman chose an earnest knight to represent virtue. He arranged for the knight to play a game of chess against a character that personified death (Bergman, 1960).

Bergman realized that some viewers might see the chess match only as an element in a complicated plot. However, he hoped that they would compare it with other sequences in the film. He hoped that they would view it as a metaphor for contests in their own lives.

ADVERTISERS

Like artists, early advertising agents relied on metaphors. They relied extensively on them when they marketed cigarettes. To increase sales, they compared male smokers to celebrities. When they later wished to sell cigarettes to females, they adapted their strategies by comparing female smokers to attractive female celebrities.

Advertisers discovered that they could convey complex messages through metaphors. However, they had to convince clients that consumers comprehended those messages. Their clients made a stipulation: they would concede that consumers comprehended marketing messages if they purchased the products and services to which those messages were connected. After agreeing to this condition, the advertisers designed marketing campaigns to increase sales. In the case of cigarettes, they were undeniably effective.

CHESS MASTERS

When persons viewed *The Seventh Seal,* they had opportunities to discern the rhetorical power of Ingmar Bergman's chess metaphor. Nonetheless, this filmmaker had made a limited observation; he had observed the similarities between chess and other situations. Some persons began to explore a novel premise; they wondered whether metaphorical activities prepared individuals for real-life problems.

Enthusiasts wondered whether the game of chess equipped individuals to excel in practical situations. They pointed out that the game nurtured skills in logic, critical thinking, and abstract reasoning. They alleged that chess players would be able to transfer those skills to other situations.

Enthusiasts claimed that numerous board games had benefits. They alleged that *Scrabble* enriched players' vocabularies, *Monopoly* increased their skills in business, and *Life* prepared them to confront marital and economic issues.

ATHLETES

Sports enthusiasts sympathized with the proponents of board games. They agreed that problems in board games prepared players for problems in life. They added that this type of learning was also a characteristic of sports.

Enthusiasts noted that the problems in sports were easy-to-comprehend because they were linked to rule-driven solutions. They contended that sporting contests were training grounds on which players prepared for more difficult-to-grasp and unwieldy problems.

The enthusiasts claimed that participation in team activities developed cooperation and leadership skills. They were equally excited about non-team sports, which they claimed developed perseverance and planning ability. They were sure that the skills developed while playing team and non-team sports transferred to other contexts.

Although advocates of sports were evident during every era, they attracted enormous publicity during World War II. They attracted the attention of politicians and military leaders, who insisted that school administrators use team sports to prepare youths for wartime service. They also attracted the attention of sports equipment manufacturers, who devised ads linking sporting triumphs to military victories (Giordano, 2004).

GAMERS

Advocates of video games agreed with the proponents of board games and sports. They were convinced that these relatively simple competitions prepared participants to solve substantive problems. They assumed that the computerized versions of board games or sporting contests would have the same attributes as the original versions.

Although some video games replicated board games or sporting contests, others had different characteristics. Games such as *Mario Brothers* involved novelties. Games such as the *Zelda* involved role-playing. Games such as *Tetris* involved puzzles. Still others involved fighting.

Street Fighter II was one of the most successful fighting games. It was the sequel to a martial arts game with a similar theme and title. Originally designed for arcades, it later was modified for home gaming consoles.

Before they were introduced to *Street Fighter II,* gamers had experimented with numerous martial arts products. They had battled heavyweight boxers, Japanese karate masters, and professional wrestlers. In spite of their experiences, they were unprepared for the innovative, inventive, and intriguing features of *Street Fighter II* (Arnold & Meston, 1994; Goddard, 1993; McDermott, Taylor, & Winstead, 1992; Taylor & Wolfe, 1994; Totally Unauthorized Guide, 1994).

Players began *Street Fighter II* by selecting a character that they would control. In an early version, they could choose from a menu with eight characters. They might select Chun Li, a female martial arts expert with speed, flexibility, and acrobatic maneuvers. However, Chun Li had a drawback: she had to strike an opponent numerous times to inflict significant damage. Players had to employ specialized tactics and strategies to win a match if they were controlling her or fighting against her.

Instead of controlling Chun Li, players might choose E. Honda. This character was an enormously strong sumo wrestler who could devastate an opponent with several punches or kicks. Nonetheless, he had a significant limitation: he had ponderously slow reactions. Players calculated that they would need specialized tactics and strategies to win matches in which they were controlling him or fighting against him.

The characters in *Street Fighter II* were distinguished by several traits. Although they all had strength, endurance, agility, and resistance to assaults, they possessed the traits in different proportions.

The characters also were distinguished by their special moves. Although all of them had these moves, they used them to summon different types of powers. Some of them hurled devastating energy balls at their opponents; others unleashed blindingly rapid sets of punches and kicks.

The developers of *Street Fighter II* marketed numerous editions of their game. Nonetheless, they did not refer to the later editions as *Street Fighter III* or *Street Fighter IV;* they continued to name the subsequent products *Street Fighter II*. Even though they left the name the same, they did change some features of the game. They introduced characters who looked more realistic, responded more rapidly, and demonstrated more fighting moves than the original characters.

Street Fighter II expanded and grew technically more elegant. In spite of these changes, it preserved the gaming dynamics of the original version. The manufacturers of other video games incorporated those sophisticated dynamics into products such as *Mortal Combat, Virtual Fighter,* and *Tekken* (Cuellar & Deats, 2005; Roberts, 1998).

Players relished the distinctive characteristics of *Street Fighter II*. They relished the opportunity to duel with other gamers; they viewed competition with live opponents as a critical dimension of video game play. They also appreciated the opportunity to compete against computer-controlled characters. They savored the challenge of picking a fighter that could confront and defeat all of the regular opponents and the arch villains that the computer matched against them.

Players treasured opportunities to learn the distinctive moves of each character in *Street Fighter II*. Although they could observe these special moves when they battled against computerized characters, they had to discover a prescribed series of control-pad commands to activate the moves when they were in charge.

Players had additional reasons for prizing *Street Fighter II*. They learned that the shrewd selection of strategies and tactics could minimize the advantages of an opposing character and compensate for the disadvantages of their own character. As a result, they could prevail with any character.

Players spent hours contemplating the art and the logic of *Street Fighter II*. They identified appropriate skills, refined them, and attempted to beat the game. They tried to transfer their skills to the problems that they faced in other video games; they also tried to transfer them to the problems that they faced in their everyday lives.

EDUCATORS

In this book, you have considered a single recurring question: how can one distinguish sound from cockeyed advice? To answer the question, you examined the advice about instructional practices, classroom materials, assessment techniques, student incentives, school facilities, and educational policies.

In addition to considering information about diverse issues, you considered information from diverse groups. For example, you weighed the recommendations of school personnel: teachers, school administrators, counselors, guidance officers, and the many specialists who collaborated with them.

You examined recommendations from the experts who explicitly investigated educational problems. You also looked at recommendations from persons who investigated other types of problems. You examined the advice of experts in philosophy, anthropology, journalism, psychology, physical therapy, animal therapy, health care, architecture, sociology, economics, and political science.

You considered one more category of information: populist recommendations. You examined the recommendations of parents, community leaders, businesspersons, military leaders, politicians, members of special interest groups, and the general public.

As you learned about the case method, you systematically applied it to information about education. Some of you applied it in groups; others used special activities to simulate group experiences.

SUMMARY

Ancient philosophers used metaphors to help their students solve problems. Modern gamers and educators who use the case method followed their lead.

References

Abdill, M. N., & Juppé, D. 1997. *Pets in therapy.* Ravensdale, WA: Idyll Arbor.

Adams, B. E. 2007. *Citizen lobbyists: Local efforts to influence public policy.* Philadelphia: Temple University Press.

Adelson, E. 2009, April 25. The principal and the paddle. *Newsweek.* Retrieved on May 4, 2009 from: http://www.newsweek.com/id/195119?Gt1=43002.

Allen, K. M. 1985. *The human-animal bond: An annotated bibliography.* Metuchen, NJ: Scarecrow Press.

American Academy of Pediatrics. 1982. Policy statement: The Doman-Delacato treatment of neurologically handicapped children. *Pediatrics, 70,* 810–812.

American Recovery and Reinvestment Act of 2009. 2009. Retrieved on 28 March, 2009 from: http://frwebgate.access.gpo.gov/cgi-bin/getdoc.cgi?dbname=111 _cong_bills&docid=f:h1enr.pdf.

Andersen, R., & Strate, L. 2000. *Critical studies in media commercialism.* New York: Oxford University Press.

Anderson, C.A.; Gentile, D.A.; & Buckley, K. E. 2007. *Violent video game effects on children and adolescents: Theory, research, and public policy.* Oxford: Oxford University Press.

Andrews, L. W. 2004. *Emotional intelligence.* New York: Watts.

Apple, M. W. 2001. *Educating the "right" way: Markets, standards, God, and inequality.* New York: Routledge.

Ariely, D. 2008. *Predictably irrational: The hidden forces that shape our decisions.* New York: Harper.

Armstrong, S. J., & Botzler, R. G. 2003. *The animal ethics reader.* London: Routledge.

Armstrong, T. 2003. *The multiple intelligences of reading and writing: Making the words come alive.* Alexandria, VA: Association for Supervision and Curriculum Development.

Arnold, J. D., & Meston, Z. 1994. *Awesome Super Nintendo secrets 4.* Lahaina, HI: Sandwich Islands.

Ascheim, S. 1973. *Materials* for *the open classroom.* New York: Dell.

Ashley, K. D. 1990. *Modeling legal argument: Reasoning with cases and hypotheticals.* Cambridge, MA: MIT Press.

Ayers, W.; Dohrn, B.; & Ayers, R. 2001. *Zero tolerance: Resisting the drive for punishment in our schools—A handbook for parents, students, educators, and citizens.* New York: New Press.

Babington, C. 2006, July 20. Stem cell bill gets Bush's first veto. *Washington Post,* p. A4. Retrieved on May 29, 2009 from: http://www.washingtonpost.com/wp-dyn/content/article/2006/07/19/AR2006071900524.html.

Baker, D. 2006, June 16. Cooking unemployment data to make the U.S. look better. *Beat the Press.* Retrieved on September 12, 2008 from: http://beatthepress.blogspot.com/2006/06/cooking-unemployment-data-to-make-us.html.

Bar-On, R.; Maree, K.; & Elias, M. J. 2007. *Educating people to be emotionally intelligent.* Westport, CN: Praeger.

Barone, D. M. 2006. *Narrowing the literacy gap: What works in high-poverty schools.* New York: Guilford.

Barrett, G. 2007, December 23. Buzzwords 2007: All we are saying. *New York Times.* Retrieved on September 12, 2008 from: http://www.nytimes.com/2007/12/23/weekinreview/23buzzwords.html?scp=2&sq=crowdsource&st=cse.

Barton, B. 2008. A tale of two case methods. *Tennessee Law Review, 75* 3. Retrieved on September 23, 2008 from: http://ssrn.com/abstract=1021306.

Baugh, J. 2000. *Beyond Ebonics: Linguistic pride and racial prejudice.* Oxford, UK: Oxford University Press.

Bausell, R. B. 2007. *Snake oil science: The truth about complementary and alternative medicine.* Oxford, UK: Oxford University Press.

Beckwith, F. 2003. *Law, Darwinism & public education: The establishment clause and the challenge of intelligent design.* Lanham, MD: Rowman & Littlefield.

Benoit, D. 2007. *The best-kept secret: Women, corporate lobbyists, policy, and power in the United States.* New Brunswick, NJ: Rutgers University Press.

Bergen, D., & Coscia, J. 2001. *Brain research and childhood education: Implications for educators.* Olney, MD: Association for Childhood Education International.

Berger, E. 2007. *Parents as partners in education: Families and schools working together* 7th edition. Englewood Cliffs, NJ: Prentice Hall.

Berger, E., & Winters, B. A. 1973. *Social studies in the open classroom: A practical guide.* New York: Teachers College Press.

Bergman, I. 1960. *Four screenplays.* New York: Simon & Schuster.

Bergman, J., & Wirth, K. H. 2008. *Slaughter of the dissidents.* Southworth, WA: Leafcutter.

Berlin, I. 2003. *Generations of captivity: A history of African-American slaves.* Cambridge, MA: Harvard University Press.

Berra, T. M. 1990. *Evolution and the myth of creationism: A basic guide to the facts in the evolution debate.* Stanford, CA: Stanford University Press.

Berube, M. R. 1991. *American presidents and education.* New York: Greenwood.

Birchall, C. 2006. *Knowledge goes pop: From conspiracy theory to gossip.* Oxford, UK: Berg.

Birnbaum, M. 2009, March 22. Stimulus cash helps county schools avoid some cuts. *Washington Post,* p. PW01. Retrieved on March 28, 2009, from: http://www .washingtonpost.com/wp-dyn/content/article/2009/03/21/AR2009032104056.html.

Bjork, D. W. 1993. *B. F. Skinner: A life.* New York: Basic Books.

Blackwell, J. 2006. *Empowering school leaders: Personal political power for school board members and administrators.* Lanham, MD: Rowman & Littlefield.

Blight, D. W. 2004. *Passages to freedom: The Underground Railroad in history and memory.* Washington, DC: Smithsonian/National Underground Railroad Freedom Center.

Blitz, B. 1973. *The open classroom: Making it work.* Boston: Allyn & Bacon.

Bloom, A. D. 1987. *The closing of the American mind: How higher education has failed democracy and impoverished the souls of today's students.* New York: Simon & Schuster.

B'nai B'rith. 1993. *Hitler's apologists: The anti-Semitic propaganda of Holocaust "revisionism."* New York: Anti-Defamation League.

Bonilla, D. M. 2000. *School violence.* New York: Wilson.

Bootel, J. A. 1995. *CEC special education advocacy handbook.* Reston, VA: Council for Exceptional Children.

Bootel, J. A. 1999. *CEC handbook for strengthening grassroots advocacy.* Reston, VA: Council for Exceptional Children.

Bosman, J. 2007, June 9. A plan to pay for top scores on some tests gains ground. *New York Times.* Retrieved on September 2, 2008 from: http://www.nytimes.com/2007/06/09/ nyregion/09schools.html?scp=3&sq=paying%20students&st=cse.

Boyd, R. S. 2009, February 1. Evolution war still rages 200 years after Darwin's birth. *Miami Herald.* Retrieved on 8 February, 2009 from: http://www.miamiherald .com/news/politics/AP/v-fullstory/story/882721.html.

Boyles, D. 2005. *Schools or markets? Commercialism, privatization, and school-business partnerships.* Mahwah, NJ: Erlbaum.

Brandt, A. M. 2007. *The cigarette century: The rise, fall, and deadly persistence of the product that defined America.* New York: Basic Books.

Bratt, B. 1989. *No time for Jell-O: One family's experience with the Doman-Delacato patterning program.* Cambridge, MA: Brookline.

Brill, S. 2003. *After: How America confronted the September 12 era.* New York: Simon & Schuster.

Brookfield, S., & Preskill, S. 1999. *Discussion as a way of teaching: Tools and techniques for democratic classrooms.* San Francisco: Jossey–Bass.

Brown, S. W., & Strong, V. 2001. The use of seizure-alert dogs. *Seizure. 10,* 39–41.

Brundage, W. F. 1997. *Under sentence of death: Lynching in the South.* Chapel Hill, NC: University of North Carolina Press.

Brunsma, D. L. 2004. *The school uniform movement and what it tells us about American education: A symbolic crusade.* Lanham, MD: ScarecrowEducation.

Brunsma, D. L. 2006. *Uniforms in public schools: A decade of research and debate.* Lanham, MD: Rowman & Littlefield.

Brunsma, D. L., & Rockquemore, K. A. 1998. Effects of student uniforms on attendance, behavior problems, substance use, and academic achievement. *Journal of Educational Research, 92* 1, 53–62.

Brunvand, J. H. 1999. *Too good to be true: The colossal book of urban legends.* New York: Norton.

Brunvand, J. H. 2004. *Be afraid, be very afraid: The book of scary urban legends.* New York: Norton.

Bryk, A.; Lee, V.; & Holland, P. 1993. *Catholic schools and the common good.* Cambridge, MA: Harvard University Press.

Buchanan, A. E., & Brock, D. W. 1989. *Deciding for others: The ethics of surrogate decision making.* Cambridge, UK: Cambridge University Press.

Bugliosi, V. 2007. *Reclaiming history: The assassination of President John F. Kennedy.* New York: Norton.

Bullough, R. V. 2001. *Uncertain lives: Children of promise, teachers of hope.* New York: Teachers College Press.

Burch, M. R. 1996. *Volunteering with your pet: How to get involved in animal-assisted therapy with any kind of pet.* New York: Howell.

Burke, N. D. 1993. Restricting gang clothing in the public schools. *West's Education Law Quarterly, 2,* 391–404.

Burnette, J. 1998. *Reducing the disproportionate representation of minority students in special education.* Reston, VA: ERIC Clearinghouse on Disabilities and Gifted Education/Council for Exceptional Children.

Califano, J. A. 1981. *Governing America: An insider's report from the White House and the cabinet.* New York: Simon & Schuster.

Califano, J. A. 2004. *Inside: A public and private life.* New York: PublicAffairs.

Capozzoli, T., & McVey, R. S. 2000. *Kids killing kids: Managing violence and gangs in schools.* Boca Raton, FL: St. Lucie.

Carper, J. 1997. *Miracle cures: Dramatic new scientific discoveries revealing the healing powers of herbs, vitamins, and other natural remedies.* New York: Harper-Collins.

Carter, J. 2005. *Our endangered values: America's moral crisis.* New York: Simon & Schuster.

Cassell, J., & Jenkins, H. Eds.. 2000. *From Barbie to Mortal Kombat: Gender and computer games.* Cambridge, MA: MIT Press.

Cell phone driving laws. 2009, May. *Governors Highway Safety Association.* Retrieved on May 12, 2009 from: http://www.ghsa.org/html/stateinfo/laws/cellphone_laws.html.

Chalmers, D. M. 2003. *Backfire: How the Ku Klux Klan helped the civil rights movement.* Lanham, MD: Rowman & Littlefield.

Chandler, C. K. 2005. *Animal assisted therapy in counseling.* New York: Routledge.

Cherniss, C., & Goleman, D. 2001. *The emotionally intelligent workplace: How to select for measure, and improve emotional intelligence in individuals, groups, and organizations.* San Francisco: Jossey–Bass.

Chesler, P. 2003. *The new anti-Semitism: The current crisis and what we must do about it.* San Francisco: Jossey–Bass.

Ciarrochi, J.; Forgas, J. P.; & Mayer, J. D. 2006. *Emotional intelligence in everyday life.* New York: Psychology Press.

Cimera, R. E. 2007. *Learning disabilities: What are they?—Helping parents and teachers understand the characteristics.* Lanham, MD: Rowman & Littlefield.

Clifford, S. 2009, May 14. Making the Sims into neighbors you can relate to. *New York Times* New York edition, p. B3. Retrieved on May 14, 2009 from: http://www.nytimes.com/2009/05/14/business/media/14adco.html?_r=1.

Clines, F. X. 1996, September 19. Spiro T. Agnew, point man for Nixon who resigned vice presidency, dies at 77. *New York Times* New York edition, p. B15. Retrieved on May 21, 2009 from: http://www.nytimes.com/1996/09/19/us/spiro-t-agnew-point-man-for-nixon-who-resigned-vice-presidency-dies-at-77.html?pagewanted=1.

Clinton, B. 2004. *My life.* New York: Knopf.

Clinton, H. R. 2003. *Living history.* New York: Simon & Schuster.

Cohen, H. J.; Birch, H. G.; & Taft, L.T. 1970. Some considerations for evaluating the Doman-Delacato "patterning" method. *Pediatrics, 45,* 302–314.

Colbert, J. A.; Desberg, P.; & Trimble, K. D. 1996. *The case for education: Contemporary approaches for using case methods.* Boston: Allyn & Bacon.

Coleman, J. S. 1991. *Parental involvement in education.* Washington, DC: United States Department of Education.

Conley, L. 2008. *OBD: Obsessive branding disorder—The business of illusion and the illusion of business.* New York: BBS/PublicAffairs.

Constantine, M. G., & Sue, D. W. 2006. *Addressing racism: Facilitating cultural competence in mental health and educational settings.* Hoboken, NJ: Wiley.

Cooper, B. S.; Cibulka, J. G.; & Fusarelli, L. D. 2008. *Handbook of education politics and policy.* New York: Routledge.

Cornett, C. E., & Cornett, C. F. 1980. *Bibliotherapy: The right book at the right time.* Bloomington, IN: Phi Delta Kappa.

Coulter, A. H. 2006. *Godless: The church of liberalism.* New York: Crown–Forum.

Crawford, J. J., & Pomerinke, K. A. 2003. *Therapy pets: The animal-human healing partnership.* Amherst, NY: Prometheus.

Cross, G. S. 2000. *An all-consuming century: Why commercialism won in modern America.* New York: Columbia University Press.

Cuellar, J., & Deats, A. 2005. *Tekken 5: Official strategy guide.* Indianapolis, IN: BradyGames.

Cummins, R. A. 1988. *The neurologically impaired-child: Doman-Delacato techniques reappraised.* London: Croom–Helm.

Cutler, W. W. 2000. *Parents and schools: The 150-year struggle for control in American education.* Chicago: University of Chicago Press.

Daly, L. 2006. *God and the welfare state.* Cambridge, MA: MIT Press.

Daniels, P. 2008. *Zero tolerance policies in schools.* Detroit: Greenhaven Press.

David, P. 1983, September 15. U.S. science education: Will Reagan foot the $830 million bill? *Nature, 305* 5931, 171.

Davies, G. 2007. *See government grow: Education politics from Johnson to Reagan.* Lawrence, KS: University Press of Kansas.

Davis, R. 2007, June 20. NYC announces plan to offer cash incentives to students. *CNN.* Retrieved on September 2, 2008 from: http://www.cnn.com/2007/EDUCATION/06/20/nyc.student.cash/index.html.

Deere, S. 2002, January 20. Cash incentives in schools debated. *Reporter—News.* Retrieved on September 2, 2008 from: http://www.texnews.com/1998/2002/local/cash0120.html.

Delacato C. H. 1963. *The diagnosis and treatment of speech and reading problems.* Springfield, IL: Charles Thomas.

DelFattore, J. 2004. *The fourth R: Conflicts over religion in America's public schools.* New Haven, CT: Yale University Press.

Devaney, L. 2009, February 17. Education snags $105.9B in stimulus package. *eSchool Journal.* Retrieved on March 28, 2009, from: http://www.eschoolnews.com/news/top-news/?i=57333.

Devinsky, O.; Schachter, S. C.; & Pacia, S. 2005. *Complementary and alternative therapies for epilepsy.* New York: Demos.

Did we land on the moon? 2009, May 5. *Rocket and Space Technology.* Retrieved on May 5, 2009 from: http://www.braeunig.us/space/hoax.htm.

Dillon, S. 2009, February 10. Trimmed bill still offers vast sums for education. *New York Times* New York edition, p. A14. Retrieved on March 28, 2009, from: http://www.nytimes.com/2009/02/10/education/10educ.html?_r=1&scp=5&sq=stimulus%20bill%20and%20education&st=cseb.

Doman, G. J. 2005. *What to do about your brain-injured child* Revised. Garden City Park, NY: Square One. Original work published in 1974.

Doman, G. J., & Doman, J. 2002. *How to teach your baby to read: The gentle revolution* Revised. Towson, MD: Gentle Revolution Press. Original work published in 1964.

Doman, G. J., & Doman, J. 2005. *How to teach your baby math* Revised. Garden City Park, NY: Square One. Original work published in 1979.

Doman, G. J., & Doman, J. 2006. *How smart is your baby? Develop and nurture your newborn's full potential.* Garden City Park, NY: Square One.

Doman, G. J.; Doman, J.; & Aisen, S. 1984. *How to give your baby encyclopedic knowledge: More gentle revolution.* Philadelphia: Better Baby Press.

Doman, R. J.; Spitz, E. B.; Zucman, E.; Delacato, C. H.; & Doman, G. J. 1960. Children with severe brain injuries: Neurological organization in terms of mobility. *Journal of the American Medical Association, 174,* 257–262.

Dowling-Sendor, B. 2002. School uniforms redux. *American School Board Journal, 189* 3, 38–39, 47.

Dray, P. 2002. *At the hands of persons unknown: The lynching of Black America.* New York: Random House.

Dudley, W. 1992. *Slavery: Opposing viewpoints.* San Diego, CA: Greenhaven Press.

Ebert, R. 2007, August 24. The King of Kong: A fistful of quarters. *RogerEbert .Com.* Retrieved on May 28, 2009 from: http://rogerebert.suntimes.com/apps/pbcs .dll/article?AID=/20070823/REVIEWS/70817011.

Eckel, P. D. 2006. *The shifting frontiers of academic decision making: Responding to new priorities, following new pathways.* Westport, CT: Praeger.

Education for All Handicapped Children Act. Pub. L. No. 94–142 1975. Retrieved on 25 August 2007 from: http://thomas.loc.gov/bss.

Egendorf, L. K. 2002. *School shootings.* San Diego, CA: Greenhaven Press

Eldredge, N. 2000. *The triumph of evolution: And the failure of creationism.* New York: Freeman.

Emery, D. 2008, April 7. Who killed Princess Diana? *About.com.* Retrieved on May, 5, 2009 from: http://urbanlegends.about.com/od/historical/a/princess_diana.htm.

Ensha, A. 2009, March 18. Traffic can give you a heart attack. *New York Times.* Retrieved on March 23, 2009 from: http://wheels.blogs.nytimes.com/2009/03/18/traffic-can -give-you-a-heart-attack/?ex=1253160000&en=6f3cb5a7d7fe2e7f&ei=5087&WT .mc_id=AU-D-I-NYT-MOD-MOD-m086-ROS-0309-HDR&WT.mc_ev=click.

Erskine, J.; Leenders, M.; & Mauffette-Leenders, L. 1998. *Teaching with cases.* London, Ontario, Canada: Ivey.

Evans, D. L. 1996. School uniforms: an "unfashionable" dissent. *Phi Delta Kappan, 78* 2, 139.

Evans, L. 2007. Public policies determine traffic deaths and fuel use. *American Journal of Public Health, 97* 4, 588.

Fader, D. N., & McNeil, E. B. 1968. *Hooked on books: Program & proof.* New York: Putnam's Sons.

Falk, A. 2008. *Anti-Semitism: A history and psychoanalysis of contemporary hatred.* Westport, CN: Praeger.

Fast, J. 2008. *Ceremonial violence: A psychological explanation of school shootings.* Woodstock, NY: Overlook.

Feagin, J. R., & McKinney, K. D. 2003. *The many costs of racism.* Lanham, MD: Rowman & Littlefield.

Fiedler, C. R., & Clark, D. 2008. *Making a difference: Advocacy competencies for special education professionals.* Austin, TX: PRO-ED.

Fine, A. H. 2000. *Handbook on animal-assisted therapy: Theoretical foundations and guidelines for practice.* San Diego: Academic Press.

Fine, A. H., & Eisen, C. J. 2008. *Afternoons with Puppy: Inspirations from a therapist and his animals.* West Lafayette, IN: Purdue University Press.

Flood, J., & Anders, P. L. 2005. *Literacy development of students in urban schools: Research and policy.* Newark, DE: International Reading Association.

Foerstel L., & Gilliam, A. Eds.. 1992. *Confronting the Margaret Mead legacy: Scholarship, empire and the South Pacific.* Philadelphia: Temple University Press.

Forrest, B., & Gross, P. R. 2004. *Creationism's Trojan horse: The wedge of intelligent design.* Oxford, UK: Oxford University Press.

Fox, R. F. 1996. *Harvesting minds: How TV commercials control kids.* Westport, CN: Praeger.

Fredrickson, G. M. 2002. *Racism: A short history.* Princeton, NJ: Princeton University Press.

Freedman, L. 2008. *A choice of enemies: America confronts the Middle East.* Philadelphia, PA: PublicAffairs.

Freeman, D. 1983. *Margaret Mead and Samoa: The making and unmaking of an anthropological myth.* Cambridge, MA: Harvard University Press.

Freeman, D. 1999. *The fateful hoaxing of Margaret Mead: A historical analysis of her Samoan research.* Boulder, CO: Westview.

Freeman, R. D. 1967. Controversy over "patterning" as a treatment for brain damage in children. *Journal of the American Medical Association, 202,* 83–86.

Freeman, S. F., & Bleifuss, J. 2006. *Was the 2004 presidential election stolen? Exit polls, election fraud, and the official count.* New York: Seven Stories.

Freire, P. 1970. *Pedagogy of the oppressed.* New York: Herder & Herder.

Freire, P. 1985. *The politics of education: Culture, power, and liberation.* South Hadley, MA: Bergin & Garvey.

Frieden, J. A. 2006. *Global capitalism: Its fall and rise in the twentieth century.* New York: Norton.

Frydenborg, K. 2006. *Animal therapist.* Philadelphia: Chelsea House.

Gabbidon, S. L. 2007. *Criminological perspectives on race and crime.* New York: Routledge.

Gabor, A. 1999. *The capitalist philosophers: The geniuses of modern business—Their lives, times, and ideas.* New York: Times Business.

Gaddy, B.; Hall, T. W.; & Marzano, R. J. 1996. *School wars: Resolving our conflicts over religion and values.* San Francisco: Jossey–Bass.

Gaither, M. 2008. *Homeschool: An American history.* New York: Palgrave–Macmillan.

Galovski, T. E.; Malta, L. S.; & Blanchard, E. B. 2006. *Road rage: Assessment and treatment of the angry, aggressive driver.* Washington, DC: American Psychological Association.

Galvin, M., & Ferraro, S. 1988. *Otto learns about his medicine: A story about medication for hyperactive children.* New York: Magination Press.

Garase, M. L. 2006. *Road rage.* New York: LFB Scholarly Publishing.

Gardner, H. 1983. *Frames of mind: The theory of multiple intelligences.* New York: Basic Books.

Gardner, H. 1999, February. Who Owns Intelligence? *Atlantic. 283* 2, 67.

Gardner, H. 2007. *Responsibility at work: How leading professionals act or don't act responsibly.* San Francisco: Jossey–Bass.

Garvin, D. A. 2000. *Learning in action.* Boston: Harvard Business School Press.

Gee, J. P. 2004. *What video games have to teach us about learning and literacy.* New York: Palgrave–Macmillan.

Gee, J. P. 2007. *Good video games and good learning: Collected essays on video games, learning and literacy.* New York: Peter Lang.

Geisler, N. L. 2007. *Creation & the courts: Eighty years of conflict in the classroom and the courtroom.* Wheaton, IL: Crossway Books.

Genge, N. 2000. *Urban legends: The as-complete-as-one-could-be guide to modern myths.* New York: Three Rivers.

Gibson, C., & Jung, K. 2002. *Historical census statistics on population totals by race, 1790 to 1990, and by Hispanic origin, 1970 to 1990, for the United States, regions, divisions, and states.* Washington, DC: United States Census Bureau. Retrieved August 7, 2007, from http://www.census.gov/population/www/documentation/twps0056.html.

Gingrich, N.; Haley, V.; & Tyler, R. 2008. *Real change: From the world that fails to the world that works.* Washington, DC: Regnery.

Giordano, G. 2000. *Twentieth-century reading education: Understanding practices of today in terms of patterns of the past.* New York: Elsevier.

Giordano, G. 2003. *Twentieth-century textbook wars: A history of advocacy and opposition.* New York: Peter Lang.

Giordano, G. 2004. *Wartime schools: How World War II changed American education.* New York: Peter Lang.

Giordano, G. 2005. *How testing came to dominate American schools: The history of educational assessment.* New York: Peter Lang.

Giordano, G. 2007. *American special education: A history of early political advocacy.* New York: Peter Lang.

Giordano, G. 2009. *Solving education problems effectively: A guide to using the case method.* Lanham, MD: Rowman & Littlefield.

Goddard, J. 1993. *Street Fighter II turbo strategy guide.* San Mateo, CA: Infotainment World.

Goldstein, A. P., & Kodluboy, D. W. 1998. *Gangs in schools: Signs, symbols, and solutions.* Champaign, IL: Research Press.

Goldwater, B. M. 1960. *The conscience of a conservative.* Shepherdsville, KY: Victor.

Goleman, D. 1995. *Emotional intelligence.* New York: Bantam Books.

Goodstein, L. 2001, January 30. Nudging church-state line, Bush invites religious groups to seek federal aid. *New York Times* New York edition, p. A18. Retrieved on May 29, 2009 from: http://www.nytimes.com/2001/01/30/us/nudging-church-state-line-bush-invites-religious-groups-to-seek-federal-aid.html?scp=9&sq=bush%20and%20faith-based%20and%20community%20organizations&st=cse.

Gootman, E. 2008, August 19. Mixed results on paying City students to pass tests. *New York Times* New York edition, p. B1. Retrieved on September 2, 2008 from: http://www.nytimes.com/2008/08/20/education/20cash.html?ref=todayspaper&pagewanted=all.

Gordon, D. T. 2003. *A nation reformed? American education 20 years after "A Nation at Risk."* Cambridge, MA: Harvard Education Press.

Gore, A. 2007. *The assault on reason.* New York: Penguin.

Gottlieb, B. 2000. *Alternative cures: The most effective natural home remedies for 160 health problems.* Emmaus, PA: Rodale.

GovTrack.us. H.R. 1—111th Congress. 2009: American Recovery and Reinvestment Act of 2009, *GovTrack.us database of federal legislation.* Retrieved on 28

March, 2009 from: http://www.govtrack.us/congress/bill.xpd?bill=h111
-1&tab=speeches.

Graham, B. 2000. *Creature comfort: Animals that heal.* Amherst, NY: Prometheus.

Grapes, B. J. 2000. *School violence.* San Diego: Greenhaven Press.

Graves, M. F.; Van Den Broek, P. W.; & Taylor, B. M. 1996. *The first R: Every child's right to read.* New York: Teachers College Press.

Greenawalt, K. 2005. *Does God belong in public schools?* Princeton, NJ: Princeton University Press.

Greenberg, K. S. 2003. *Nat Turner: A slave rebellion in history and memory.* Oxford, UK: Oxford University Press.

Gross, J. T. 2006. *Fear: Anti-Semitism in Poland after Auschwitz: An essay in historical interpretation.* New York: Random House.

Grossman, H. 1998. *Ending discrimination in special education.* Springfield, IL: Charles Thomas.

Guernsey, L. 2008, March 3. Reward for students under a microscope. *New York Times.* Retrieved on March 3, 2009 from: http://www.nytimes.com/2009/03/03/health/03rewa.html.

Guyer, P. 2006. *Kant.* London: Routledge.

Haldeman, E. G., & Idstein, S. 1977. *Bibliotherapy.* Washington, DC: University Press of America.

Harris, T. 2001, May 16. How urban legends work. *HowStuffWorks.com.* Retrieved on October 23, 2008 from: http://people.howstuffworks.com/urban-legend.htm.

Harrison, B. 2006. *The resurgence of anti-Semitism: Jews, Israel, and liberal opinion.* Lanham, MD: Rowman & Littlefield.

Hartley, R. F. 1990. *Marketing successes, historical to present day: What we can learn.* New York: Wiley.

Hartman, J. L. 2009, January 24. What's inside the stimulus package for education? *Oh My Gov!* Retrieved on March 28, 2009, from: http://ohmygov.com/blogs/general_news/archive/2009/01/24/what-s-in-the-stimulus-package-for-education.aspx.

Haugen, D. M. 2008. *Alternative medicine.* Detroit: Greenhaven Press.

Hayes, W. 2004. *Are we still a nation at risk two decades later?* Lanham, MD: ScarecrowEducation.

Hernandez, J. C. 2008, September 25. New effort aims to test theories of education. *New York Times* New York edition, p. B6. Retrieved on September 25, 2008 from: http://www.nytimes.com/2008/09/25/education/25educ.html?_r=1&ref=todayspaper&oref=slogin.

Herreid, C. F. 2007. *Start with a story: The case study method of teaching college science.* Arlington, VA: National Science Teachers Association.

Hertzberg, A., & Stone, E. F. 1971. *Schools are for children: An American approach to the open classroom.* New York: Schocken.

High gas prices cause surge in motorcycle sales. 2008, August 19. *US News & World Report.* Retrieved on September 12, 2008 from: http://usnews.rankingsandreviews.com/cars-trucks/daily-news/080819-High-Gas-Prices-Cause-Surge-in-Motorcycle-Sales/.

Hoffer, E. 1951. *The true believer: Thoughts on the nature of mass movements.* New York: Harper & Row.

Hoffman, M. 1978. *Vermont diary: Language arts in the open classroom.* New York: Teachers & Writers.

Hold the line on school reform. 2009, April9. *New York Times* New York edition, p. A26. Retrieved on April 10, 2009 from: http://www.nytimes.com/2009/04/09/opinion/09thu2.html?ref=opinion.

Holmes, L. D. 1987. *Quest for the real Samoa: the Mead/Freeman controversy & beyond.* South Hadley, MA: Bergin & Garvey.

Horowitz, D. 2006. *The professors: The 101 most dangerous academics in America.* Washington, DC: Regnery.

Horowitz, D. 2007. *Indoctrination U.: The left's war against academic freedom.* New York: Encounter.

Horton, J. O., & Horton, L. E. 2005. *Slavery and the making of America.* Oxford, UK: Oxford University Press.

Howe, J. 2006, June. The rise of crowdsourcing. *Wired.* Retrieved on December 22, 2008 from: http://www.wired.com/wired/archive/14.06/crowds.html?pg=1&topic=crowds&topic_set.

Howe, J. 2008. *Crowdsourcing: Why the power of the crowd is driving the future of business.* New York: Crown.

Howell, J. C., & Lynch, J. P. 2000. *Youth gangs in schools.* Washington, DC: Department of Justice.

Howes, V. M. 1974. *Informal teaching in the open classroom.* New York: Macmillan.

Hudson, D. L. 2004. *Rights of students.* Philadelphia: Chelsea House.

Hunnicutt, S. 2006. *School shootings.* Farmington Hills, MI: Greenhaven Press/Thomson–Gale.

Hunter, M. 1982, August 11. Congress balking at Reagan plan for disabled. *New York Times.* Retrieved on April 4, 2009 from: http://www.nytimes.com/1982/08/11/us/congress-balking-at-reagan-plan-for-disabled.html.

Huston, J., & Traven, B. 1979. *The treasure of the Sierra Madre.* Madison, WI: University of Wisconsin Press. Original screenplay published in 1947; film released in 1948.

Hutt, S. J. 1989. *Play, exploration, and learning: A natural history of the pre-school.* London: Routledge.

Institute for Intergovernmental Research. 2009. *Compilation of gang-related legislation.* Retrieved on 6 February 2009 from: http://www.iir.com/nygc/gang-legis/default.htm.

Irlen, H. 1991. *Reading by the colors: Overcoming dyslexia and other reading disabilities through the Irlen method.* Garden City Park, NY: Avery.

Irlen, H. 1998. *Irlen: A piece of the puzzle for reading problems, learning difficulties, ADD/HD, dyslexia, headaches, and other physical symptom through the use of color.* Retrieved on 13 February, 2009 from: http://irlen.com/index.php?s=about.

Jain, A. K. 2008. *Decision sheet and learning diary: New tools for improved learning through the case method.* Ahmedabad, India: Indian Institute of Management.

James, P. 2001. *The murderous paradise: German nationalism and the Holocaust.* Westport, CN: Praeger.

Jenkins, H. 2006. *Fans, bloggers, and gamers: Exploring participatory culture.* New York: New York University Press.

Jeynes, W. 2002. *Divorce, family structure, and the academic success of children.* New York: Haworth.

Johnson, S. 2006. *Everything bad is good for you.* New York: Riverhead.

Jones, A. 2009, May 26 How much wind is in your hair depends on the state you're in. *Kalamazoo Gazette.* Retrieved on 28 May 2009 from: http://www.mlive.com/business/west-michigan/index.ssf/2009/05/how_much_wind_is_in_your_hair.html.

Jurcisin G. 1968. Dynamics of the Doman-Delacato creeping-crawling technique for the brain-damaged child. *American Corrective Therapy Journal, 22* 5, 161–164.

Kalyanpur, M., & Harry, B. 1999. *Culture in special education: Building reciprocal family-professional relationships.* Baltimore, MD: Paul Brookes.

Kanigel, R. 1997. Th*e one best way: Frederick Winslow Taylor and the enigma of efficiency.* New York: Viking.

Kennedy, J. F. 1964. *Profiles in courage.* New York: Harper & Row. Original work published in 1955.

Kennedy, W. D. 2003. *Myths of American slavery.* Gretna, LA: Pelican.

Kent, D. 2003. *Animal helpers for the disabled.* New York: Watts.

Kincheloe, J. L. 2007. *Urban education: A comprehensive guide for educators, parents, and teachers.* Lanham, MD: Rowman & Littlefield.

Kincheloe, J. L., & Steinberg, S. R. 2007. *Cutting class: Socioeconomic status and education.* Lanham, MD: Rowman & Littlefield.

Kirkpatrick, D. D. 2008, October 12. The long run: Writing memoir, McCain found a narrative for life. *New York Times* New York edition, p. A1. Retrieved on October 23, 2008 from: http://www.nytimes.com/2008/10/13/us/politics/13mccain.html?_r=1&scp=4&sq=Salter&st=cse&oref=slogin.

Kitch, C. L. 2001. *The girl on the magazine cover: The origins of visual stereotypes in American mass media.* Chapel Hill, NC: University of North Carolina Press.

Kohl, H. R. 1969. The *open classroom: A practical guide to a new way of teaching.* New York: Random House.

Kohl, H. R. 1974. *Math, writing & games: In the open classroom.* New York: Random House.

Kohn, A. 1998. *What to look for in a classroom and other essays.* San Francisco: Jossey-Bass.

Kolata, G. 1998, December 6. Scientific myths that are too good to die. *New York Times.* Retrieved on September 12, 2008 from: http://query.nytimes.com/gst/fullpage.html?res=9B06E1DB1E3BF935A35751C1A96E958260&sec=&spon=&pagewanted=all.

Kraus, J. R., & Martin, W. 2005. *Cory stories: A kid's book about living with ADHD.* Washington, DC: Magination Press.

Kroth, R. L.; Edge, D.; & Kroth, R. L. 1997. *Strategies for communicating with parents and families of exceptional children.* Denver, CO: Love.

Kuehn, M. 2001. *Kant: A biography.* New York: Cambridge University Press.

Kunzman, R. 2006. *Grappling with the good: Talking about religion and morality in public schools.* Albany, NY: State University of New York Press.

Kuo, J. D. 2006. *Tempting faith: An inside story of political seduction.* New York: Free Press.

Kutner, L., & Olson, C. K. 2008. *Grand theft childhood: The surprising truth about violent video games and what parents can do.* New York: Simon & Schuster.

Lagorce, A. 2003, September 25. Low-carb beer fattens Anheuser Busch. *Forbes .com.* Retrieved on 9 February 9, 2009 from: http://www.forbes.com/2003/09/25/cx_al_0925bud.html.

Lal, S. R.; Lal, D.; & Achilles, C. M. 1993. *Handbook on gangs in schools: Strategies to reduce gang-related activities.* Thousand Oaks, CA: Corwin Press.

Lapp, D. 2004. *Teaching all the children: Strategies for developing literacy in an urban setting.* New York: Guilford.

Laqueur, W. 2006. *The changing face of anti-Semitism: From ancient times to the present day.* New York: Oxford University Press.

Larson, C. A. 2007. *Alternative medicine.* Westport, CO: Greenwood.

Larson, E. J. 2003. *Trial and error: The American controversy over creation and evolution.* New York: Oxford University Press.

Lassetter, K. 2009. Do road signs and billboards really contribute to car accidents? *Street Diretory.com.* Retrieved on May 12, 2009 from: http://www.streetdirectory.com/travel_guide/12670/car_accidents/do_road_signs_and_billboards_really_contribute_to_car_accidents.html.

Lazear, D. G. 1994. *Multiple intelligence approaches to assessment: Solving the assessment conundrum.* Tucson, AZ: Zephyr Press.

Leland, J., & Joseph, N. 1997. Education: Hooked on Ebonics. *Newsweek, 129* 2, 78–79.

Lenhart, A.; Kahne, J.; Middaugh, E.; Macgill, A.; Evans, C.; & Vitak, J. 2008, September 16. Teens, video games and civics. *Pew Internet.* Retrieved on June 18, 2009 from: http://www.pewinternet.org/Reports/2008/Teens-Video-Games-and-Civics.aspx.

Lent, J. A. Ed.. 1999. *Pulp demons: International dimensions of the postwar anti-comics campaign.* Madison, NJ: Farleigh Dickinson University Press.

Leonard, C. 2009, June 6. For many workers, fear of layoff is big motivator. *Kansas City Star.* Retrieved on June 8, 2009 from: http://www.kansascity.com/438/story/1237142.html.

Levy, A. 2005. *The first emancipator: The forgotten story of Robert Carter, the founding father who freed his slaves.* New York: Random House.

Levy, R. 1984. Mead, Freeman, and Samoa: The problem of seeing things as they are. *Ethos, 12* 1, 85–92.

Lewin-Benham, A. 2006. *Possible schools: The Reggio approach to urban education.* New York: Teachers College Press.

Lewkowicz, A. B. 2007. *Teaching emotional intelligence: Strategies and activities for helping students make effective choices.* Thousand Oaks, CA: Corwin Press.

Lipstadt, D. E. 1993. *Denying the Holocaust: The growing assault on truth and memory.* New York: Free Press.

Locke, J. 1947. *On politics and education.* New York: Black. Original work published in 1714.

Loesch, P. C. 1995. A school uniform program that works. *Principal, 74* 4, 28–30.

Losen, D. J., & Orfield, G. 2002. *Racial inequity in special education.* Cambridge, MA: Harvard Education Press.

Lund, L. 1993. *Ten years after A Nation at Risk.* New York: Conference Board.

Lyman, L. L., & Villani, C. J. 2004. *Best leadership practices for high-poverty schools.* Lanham, MD: ScarecrowEducation.

Mackenzie, E. R., & Rakel, B. 2006. *Complementary and alternative medicine for older adults: A guide to holistic approaches to healthy aging.* New York: Springer.

MacLean, N. 1994. *Behind the mask of chivalry: The making of the second Ku Klux Klan.* New York: Oxford University Press.

Maczulak, A. E. 2007. *The five-second rule and other myths about germs: What everyone should know about bacteria, viruses, mold, and mildew.* New York: Thunder's Mouth.

Manos, M. A. 2006. *Knowing where to draw the line: Ethical and legal standards for best classroom practice.* Westport, CN: Praeger.

Marche, S. 2009, April 21. Why people who love conspiracy theories are part of the problem. *Esquire.* Retrieved on May 19, 2009 from: http://www.esquire.com/features/thousand-words-on-culture/conspiracy-theories-0509.

Marich, R. 2005. *Marketing to moviegoers: A handbook of strategies used by major studios and independents.* Burlington, MA: Elsevier.

Markowitz, J. 1996. *Disproportionate representation a critique of state and local strategies.* Alexandria, VA: National Association of State Directors of Special Education.

Markowitz, J.; Garcia, S. B.; & Eichelberger, J. H. 1997. *Addressing the disproportionate representation of students from racial and ethnic minority groups in special education: A resource document.* Alexandria, VA: National Association of State Directors of Special Education.

Marx, K., & Engels, F. 1848. *Manifesto of the Communist Party.* Retrieved on 23 October 2008 from: http://www.anu.edu.au/polsci/marx/classics/manifesto.html.

Matthews, C. 1988. *Hardball: How politics is played—Told by one who knows the game.* New York: Summit.

Matthews, G.; Zeidner, M.; & Roberts, R. D. 2007. *The science of emotional intelligence: Knowns and unknowns.* Oxford, UK: Oxford University Press.

Mayer, J. 2008. *The dark side: The inside story of how the war on terror turned into a war on American ideals.* New York: Doubleday.

Mayor, S. 2007. Report recommends tighter legislation and better road design to reduce traffic injuries and deaths. *British Medical Journal, 334,* 7599.

McAndrews, L. J. 2006. *The era of education: The presidents and the schools, 1965–2001.* Urbana, IL: University of Illinois Press.

McCain, J., & Salter, M. 2007. *Hard call: Great decisions and the extraordinary people who made them.* New York: Twelve.

McCall, J. M. 2007. *Viewer discretion advised: Taking control of mass media influences.* Lanham, MD: Rowman & Littlefield.

McDermott, L.; Taylor, M.; & Winstead, D. 1992. *Street Fighter II strategy guide.* San Mateo, CA: GamePro.

McDonald, M. A., & Milne, G. R. 1999. *Cases in sport marketing.* Sudbury, MA: Jones & Bartlett.

McMillan G. P, & Lapham, S. 2006. Effectiveness of bans and laws in reducing traffic deaths: Legalized Sunday packaged alcohol sales and alcohol-related traffic crashes and crash fatalities in New Mexico. *American Journal of Public Health,* 96 11, 1944–1948.

McNamara, M. 2006, January 12. Dogs excel in cancer-sniff study. *CBS News.* Retrieved on September 25, 2008 from: http://www.cbsnews.com/stories/2006/01/12/health/webmd/main1204680.shtml.

McNeil, M. 2009, April 1. States eye education stimulus to fill budget gaps. *Education Week,* pp 1, 24. Retrieved on March 28, 2009, from: http://www.edweek.org/ew/articles/2009/03/27/27formula.h28.html.

Mead, M. 1961. *Coming of age in Samoa: A psychological study of primitive youth for Western civilization.* New York: Morrow. Original work published in 1928.

Mennin, S.; Schwartz, P.; & Webb, G. 2001. *Problem-based learning: Case studies, experience and practice.* London, UK: Kogan–Page.

Mertz, K., & Weiss, H. 2008. Changes in motorcycle-related head injury deaths, hospitalizations, and hospital charges following repeal of Pennsylvania's mandatory motorcycle helmet law. *American Journal of Public Health, 98* 8, 1464–1467.

Mikkelson, B., & Mikkelson, D. 2007, February 27. Belle pepper. *Urban Legends References Pages.* Retrieved on May 5, 2009 from: http://www.snopes.com/business/secret/drpepper.asp.

Miller, K. D. 2008. *Choices in breast cancer treatment: Medical specialists and cancer survivors tell you what you need to know.* Baltimore: Johns Hopkins University Press.

Minorities more likely to be paddled—While corporal punishment in schools is declining, racial disparity persists. 2008, August 20. *MSNBC.* Retrieved on September 2, 2008 from: http://www.msnbc.msn.com/id/26297991.

Mitchell, A. 1996, February 25. Clinton will advise schools on uniforms. *New York Times.* Retrieved on September 12, 2008 from: http://query.nytimes.com/gst/fullpage.html?res=9C05E4DF1139F936A15751C0A960958260&sec=&spon=&pagewanted=all.

Moe, T. M. 2001. *Schools, vouchers, and the American public.* Washington, DC: Brookings Institute.

Moerman, D. E. 2002. *Meaning, medicine, and the "placebo effect."* Cambridge, UK: Cambridge University Press.

Moore, M. 2003. *Dude, where's my country?* New York: Warner.

Morales, L. 2008, June 27. Americans prioritize the economy over terrorism: Majority viewpoint persists across all incomes and among independents. *Gallup.* Retrieved on May 21, 2009 from: http://www.gallup.com/poll/108415/Americans-Prioritize -Economy-Over-Terrorism.aspx.

Morçöl, G. 2007. *Handbook of decision making.* Boca Raton, FL: Taylor & Francis.

More than half of all traffic deaths in the world happen in Asia. 2004. *Far Eastern Economic Review, 167,* 30–33.

Morgan, L. L.; Richman, V. C.; & Taylor, A. B. 1981. *Beyond the open classroom: Toward informal education.* Saratoga, CA: Century Twenty One.

Morris, H. M. 1985. *Scientific creationism.* El Cajon, CA: Master Books.

Moss, D. M., & Schwartz, C. 1989. *Shelley, the hyperactive turtle.* Kensington, MD: Woodbine House.

Moss, P. A. 2007. *Evidence and decision making.* Chicago, IL: National Society for the Study of Education.

Motorcycle deaths among boomers raise concerns. 2005, January 22. *USA Today.* Retrieved on September 12, 2008 from: http://www.usatoday.com/money/ autos/2005-01-22-motorcycle-deaths_x.htm.

Murphy, K. R. Ed.. 2006. *A critique of emotional intelligence: What are the problems and how can they be fixed?* Mahwah, NJ: Erlbaum.

Murray, J. 2009. *Therapy animals.* Edina, MN: ABDO.

Nagel, D. 2009, February. Package signed into law—What it means for K-12 education. *THE Journal.* Retrieved on March 28, 2009, from: http://www.thejournal .com/articles/23982.

Nagourney, E. 2008, December 22. Patterns: More sleep, few student car accidents. *New York Times* New York edition, p. D6. Retrieved on December 22, 2008 from: http://www.nytimes.com/2008/12/23/health/23patt.html?ref=todayspaper.

National Center for Statistics and Analysis. 1998. *Further analysis of motor- cycle helmet effectiveness using CODES linked data.* Washington, DC: National Highway Traffic Safety Administration.

National Commission on Excellence in Education. 1983. *A nation at risk: The imperative for educational reform.* Washington, DC: United States Department of Education.

National School Boards Association. 1995. *Advocacy toolkit: A "how-to" guide to powerful education advocacy.* Alexandria, VA: Author.

Neuman, S. B. 2008. *Educating the other America: Top experts tackle poverty, literacy, and achievement in our schools.* Baltimore, MD: Paul Brookes.

Newman, K. S. 2004. *Rampage: The social roots of school shootings.* New York: Basic Books.

Newport, F. 2008, June 20. Republicans, Democrats differ on creationism. *Gallup Daily.* Retrieved on 8 February, 2009 from: http://www.gallup.com/poll/108226/ Republicans-Democrats-Differ-Creationism.aspx.

Nichols, J. 2006. *The genius of impeachment: The founders' cure for royalism—And why it must be applied to George W. Bush.* New York: New Press.

Nixon, R. M. 1978. *RN: The memoirs of Richard Nixon.* New York: Grosset & Dunlap.

Nownes, A. J. 2006. *Total lobbying: What lobbyists want and how they try to get it.* New York: Cambridge University Press.

Number 23 frequency enigma. 2009. *Numerologist.com.* Retrieved on March 12, 2009 from: http://afgen.com/numbr23b.html.

Nyberg, A. K. 1998. *Seal of approval: The history of the comics code.* Jackson, MS: University Press of Mississippi.

NYC drivers named America's most aggressive. June 16, 2009. *MSNBC.* Retrieved on June 16, 2009 from: http://www.msnbc.msn.com/id/31380857/ns/us_news-life.

Obama, B. 2006. *The audacity of hope: Thoughts on reclaiming the American dream.* New York: Crown.

O'Donohue, W. T., & Ferguson, K. E. 2001. *The psychology of B. F. Skinner.* Thousand Oaks, CA: Sage.

Ohanian, S. 2001. *Caught in the middle: Nonstandard kids and a killing curriculum.* Portsmouth, NH: Heinemann.

Oliver, C. 1999. *Animals helping with special needs.* New York: Watts.

Olson, R.; Verley, J.; Santos, L.; & Salas, C. 2004. What we teach students about the Hawthorne studies: A review of content with a sample of I-O and OB textbooks. *Industrial-Organizational Psychologist, 41* 3, 23–39.

Orans, M. 1996. *Not even wrong: Margaret Mead, Derek Freeman, and the Samoans.* Novato, CA: Chandler & Sharp.

O'Reilly, B. 2001. *The no spin zone: Confrontations with the powerful and famous in America.* New York: Broadway.

Osagie, I. F. 2000. *The Amistad revolt: Memory, slavery, and the politics of identity in the United States and Sierra Leone.* Athens, GA: University of Georgia Press.

Owens, M. L. 2007. *God and government in the ghetto: The politics of church-state collaboration in Black America.* Chicago: University of Chicago Press.

Paley, A. R. 2007, February 6. New spending for No Child Left Behind. *Washington Post,* p. A07. Retrieved on May 21, 2009 from: http://www.washingtonpost.com/wp-dyn/content/article/2007/02/05/AR2007020501442.html.

Palfrey, J., & Gasser, U. 2008. *Born digital: Understanding the first generation of digital natives.* New York: Basic Books.

Parker, M., & Parish, J. 2001. *The age of anxiety: Conspiracy theory and the human sciences.* Oxford, UK: Blackwell.

Pavlides, M. 2008. *Animal-assisted interventions for individuals with autism.* London: Kingsley.

Pennock, P. E. 2007. *Advertising sin and sickness: The politics of alcohol and tobacco marketing, 1950–1990.* DeKalb, IL: Northern Illinois University Press.

Perlstcin, R. 2001. *Before the storm: Barry Goldwater and the unmaking of the American consensus.* New York: Hill & Wang.

Perry, T., & Delpit, L. D. 1998. *The real Ebonics debate: Power, language, and the education of African-American children.* Boston: Beacon.

Peterson, P. E., & Chubb, J. E. 2003. *Our schools and our future: Are we still at risk?* Stanford, CA: Hoover Institution Press.

Philp, R. 2007. *Engaging tweens and teens: A brain-compatible approach to reaching middle and high school students.* Thousand Oaks, CA: Corwin Press.

Pichot, T., & Coulter, M. 2007. *Animal-assisted brief therapy: A solution-focused approach.* New York: Haworth.

Pincas, S., & Loiseau, M. 2008. *A history of advertising.* Köln, Germany: Taschen.

Plato. 1941. *Plato's the Republic* B. Jowett, Trans.. New York: Modern Library. Original work published in 360 BCE.

Poole, I. J. 2005. Biker Brigade: Motorcycle deaths are on the rise, but states aren't pushing hard to toughen helmet laws. *Congressional Quarterly Weekly, 63* 20, 1287–1288.

Prensky, M. 2006. *Don't bother me mom—I'm learning!* New York: Paragon.

Prensky, M. 2007. *Digital game-based learning.* New York: Paragon.

President Reagan's 1984 education budget. 1983, February 9. *Education Week.* Retrieved on 29 March, 2009 from: http://www.edweek.org/ew/articles/1983/02/09/03070013.h02.html.

Princiotta, D.; Bielick, S.; & Chapman, C. 2006. *Homeschooling in the United States, 2003.* Washington, DC: United States Department of Education.

Pusillanimous pastors are worse than strident atheists. 2007, November 5. *Conservative Truth.* Retrieved on 29 March, 2009 from: http://www.pastormarkmitchell.org/?p=30.

Quart, A. 2003. *Branded: The buying and selling of teenagers.* Cambridge, MA: Perseus.

Rabin, R. L., & Sugarman, S. D. 2001. *Regulating tobacco.* Oxford, UK: Oxford University Press.

Ramirez, J. D. 2005. *Ebonics: The urban education debate.* New perspectives on language and education. Clevedon, Hants, UK: Multilingual Matters.

Rana, F. 2008. *The cell's design: How chemistry reveals the Creator's artistry.* Grand Rapids, MI: Baker.

Randrup, N., & Sekits, A. 2007. *The case method: Road map for how best to study, analyze and present cases* 2nd ed.. Rodovre, Denmark: International Management Press.

Rathbone, C. 1971. *Open education: The informal classroom—A selection of readings that examine the practices and principles of the British infant schools and their American counterparts.* New York: Citation.

Rattansi, A. 2007. *Racism: A very short introduction.* Oxford, UK: Oxford University Press.

Ravitch, D., & Viteritti, J. P. 1997. *New schools for a new century: The redesign of urban education.* New Haven, CN: Yale University Press.

Reagan backs bill limiting courts in prayer suits 1982, September 15. *Education Week.* Retrieved on March 28, 2009, from: http://www.edweek.org/ew/articles/1982/09/15/02050014.h02.html.

Reagan, R. 1990. *An American life.* New York: Simon & Schuster.

Reagan, R., & Brinkley, D. 2007. *The Reagan diaries.* New York: HarperCollins.

Reinhold, R. 1982, May 13. Reagan warns schools are failing to meet science and math needs. *New York Times.* Retrieved on March 28, 2009, from: http://www .nytimes.com/1982/05/13/us/reagan-warns-schools-are-failing-to-meet-science -and-math-needs.html?sec=technology&&n=Top/Reference/Times%20Topics/ Subjects/E/Education%20and%20Schools.

Reyes, A. H. 2006. *Discipline, achievement, and race: Is zero tolerance the answer?* Lanham, MD: Rowman & Littlefield.

Rivero, L. 2008. *The homeschooling option: How to decide when it's right for your family.* New York: Palgrave–Macmillan.

Roberts, N. 1998. *Nintendo 64 game secrets—Unauthorized* Vol. 3. Rocklin, CA: Prima.

Roeper, R. 2008. *Debunked!—Conspiracy theories, urban legends, and evil plots of the 21st century.* Chicago: Chicago Review.

Romano, R. C., & Raiford, L. 2006. *The Civil Rights Movement in American memory.* Athens, GA: University of Georgia Press.

Ronson, J. 2002. *Them: Adventures with extremists.* New York: Simon & Schuster.

Rosen, E. 2000. *The anatomy of buzz: How to create word-of-mouth marketing.* New York: Random House.

Rosenbaum, R. 2004. *Those who forget the past: The question of anti-Semitism.* New York: Random House.

Rothstein, S. W. 1994. *Schooling the poor: A social inquiry into the American educational experience.* Westport, CN: Bergin & Garvey.

Rounds, S. 1975. *Teaching the young child: A handbook of open classroom practice.* New York: Agathon.

Rozell, M. J., & Whitney, G. 2007. *Religion and the Bush presidency.* New York: Palgrave–Macmillan.

Rubin, R. J. 1978. *Bibliotherapy sourcebook.* Phoenix, AZ: Oryx.

Russell-Brown, K. 2006. *Protecting our own: Race, crime, and African Americans.* Lanham, MD: Rowman & Littlefield.

Rylant, C., & Schindler, S. D. 1985. *Every living thing: Stories.* New York: Bradbury.

Sabaroff, R. E., & Hanna, M. A. 1974. *The open classroom: A practical guide for the teacher of the elementary grades.* Metuchen, NJ: Scarecrow Press.

Samuels, C. A. 2009, April 1. Stimulus providing big funding boost for early childhood. *Education Week,* p. 8. Retrieved on March 28, 2009, from: http://www .edweek.org/ew/articles/2009/04/01/27early.h28.html.

Schaler, J. A. 2006. *Howard Gardner under fire.* Chicago, IL: Open–Court.

Schiesel, S. 2008a, April 16. Exploring fantasy life and finding a $4 billion franchise. *New York Times.* Retrieved on 4 September 2009 from: http://www.nytimes .com/2008/04/16/arts/television/16sims.html?scp=4&sq=sims&st=nyt.

Schiesel, S. 2008b, April 28. Grand Theft Auto takes on New York. *New York Times.* Retrieved on 4 September 2009 from: http://www.nytimes.com/2008/04/28/ arts/28auto.html?_r=1&th&emc=th&oref=slogin.

Schiesel, S. 2009, February 26. An industry is booming, but not just for gamers. *New York Times*. Retrieved on 4 September 2009 from: http://www.nytimes .com/2009/02/25/arts/television/25video.html?_r=2&ref=todayspaper.

Schlesinger, R. 2008. *White House ghosts: Presidents and their speechwriters*. New York: Simon & Schuster.

Schoen, A. M. 2001. *Kindred spirits: How the remarkable bond between humans and animals can change the way we live*. New York: Broadway.

Seelye, K. O. 2008, March 24. Clinton 'misspoke' about Bosnia trip. *New York Times*. Retrieved on May 4, 2009 from: http://thecaucus.blogs.nytimes.com/2008/03/24/ clinton-misspoke-about-bosnia-trip-campaign-says/.

Sepkowitz, K. A. 2008, September 7. *No need for speed*. Retrieved on September 12, 2008 from: http://www.nytimes.com/2008/09/08/opinion/08sepkowitz .html?ref=opinion.

Shaffer, D. W. 2006. *How computer games help children learn*. New York: Palgrave–Macmillan.

Sharp, D., & Bergman, J. 2008. *Persuaded by the evidence: True stories of faith, science, & the power of a creator*. Green Forest, AR: Master.

Shea, T. M., & Bauer, A. M. 1994. *Learners with disabilities: A social systems perspective of special education*. Madison, WI: Brown & Benchmark.

Shermer, M., & Grobman, A. 2000. *Denying history: Who says the Holocaust never happened and why do they say it?* Berkeley, CA: University of California Press.

Sieff, M. 2008, October 20. Obama, McCain play fear factor in presidential race. *UPI.Com*. Retrieved on May 21, 2009 from: http://www.upi.com/news/ issueoftheday/2008/10/20/Obama-McCain-play-Fear-Factor-in-presidential-race/ UPI-73981224520141/.

Siegel, B. 2003. *Helping children with autism learn: Treatment approaches for parents and professionals*. Oxford, UK: Oxford University Press.

Silberman, C. E. 1973. *The open classroom reader*. New York: Random House.

Silver, H., & Silver, P. 1991. *An educational war on poverty: American and British policy-making, 1960–1980*. Cambridge, UK: Cambridge University Press.

Skinner, B. F. 1968. *The technology of teaching*. New York: Appleton–Century–Crofts.

Skinner, B. F., & Epstein, R. 1982. *Skinner for the classroom: Selected papers*. Champaign, IL: Research Press.

Skinner, B. F., & Krakower, S. A. 1968. *Handwriting with write and see*. Chicago: Lyons & Carnahan.

Slater, W. 2009, May 27. Texas faith: When is it okay to use God to advance public policy? *Dallas News*. Retrieved on May 29, 2009 from: http://religionblog .dallasnews.com/archives/2009/05/texas-faith-when-is-it-okay-to.html.

Slavin, R. E., & Madden, N. A. 2001. *Success for all: Research and reform in elementary education*. Mahwah, NJ: Erlbaum.

Smilkstein, R. 2003. *We're born to learn: Using the brain's natural learning process to create today's curriculum*. Thousand Oaks, CA: Corwin Press.

Smith, L. L. 1974. *Jack out of the box: A practical guide to the open classroom*. West Nyack, NY: Parker.

Snyder, M., & Lindquist, R. 1998. *Complementary/alternative therapies in nursing.* New York: Springer.

Sorgel, M. 2009, February 8. Wise to introduce intelligent design bill. *Florida Times-Union,* pp. A1, A11.

Spencer D. C. 2007. Understanding seizure dogs. *Neurology, 68* 4, 2–3.

Spender, J. C., & Kijne, H. J. 1996. *Scientific management: Frederick Winslow Taylor's gift to the world?* Boston: Kluwer.

Stein, S. J. 2004. *The culture of education policy.* New York: Teachers College Press.

Steinhauser, P. 2008, September 23. CNN poll: GOP takes brunt of blame for economy. *CNNPolitics.Com.* Retrieved on May 21, 2009 from: http://www.cnn.com/2008/POLITICS/09/22/cnn.poll/.

Stella, J.; Cooke, C.; & Sprivulis, P. 2002. Most head injury related motorcycle crash deaths are related to poor riding practices. *Emergency Medicine, 14* 1, 58–61.

Stern, K. S. 1993. *Holocaust denial.* New York: American Jewish Committee.

Stern, S. 2003. *Breaking free: Public school lessons and the imperative of school choice.* San Francisco: Encounter.

Stimulus package and education funding. 2009, February 15. *Destin Spaces Blog.* Retrieved on March 28, 2009, from: http://atd.agranite.com/emerald-coast/education/stimulus-package-and-education-funding/.

Stossel J., & Binkley G. 2007, May 3. Can a penny dropped from a building kill a pedestrian below? *ABC News.* Retrieved on May, 5, 2009 from: http://abcnews.go.com/2020/story?id=3131332&page=1.

Surowiecki, J. 2004. *The wisdom of crowds: Why the many are smarter than the few and how collective wisdom shapes business, economies, societies, and nations.* New York: Doubleday.

Suskind, R. 2006. *The one percent doctrine: Deep inside America's pursuit of its enemies since 9/11.* New York: Simon & Schuster.

Szalavitz, M. 2007. The trouble with troubled teen programs: How the "boot camp" industry tortures and kills kids. *Reason, 38* 8, 48–57.

Taylor, G. R. 2004. *Parenting skills and collaborative services for students with disabilities.* Lanham, MD: ScarecrowEducation.

Taylor, J. 1971. *Organizing and integrating the infant day.* London: Allen & Unwin

Taylor, J. 1972. *Organizing the open classroom: A teachers' guide to the integrated day.* New York: Schocken.

Taylor, M., & Wolfe, G. 1994. *Super Street Fighter II: Official players guide.* San Mateo, CA: Infotainment World.

Thibadeau, G. 1976. *Opening up education: A theoretical and practical guide to the open classroom.* Dubuque, IA: Kendall–Hunt.

Thomas, E. W., & LeWinn, E. B. 1969. *Brain-injured children, with special reference to Doman-Delacato methods of treatment.* Springfield, IL: Charles Thomas.

Thomas, J. I. 1975. *Learning centers: Opening up the classroom.* Boston: Holbrook.

Thomas, L. 1993. *Vessels of evil: American slavery and the Holocaust.* Philadelphia: Temple University Press.

Thomas, R. M. 2007. *God in the classroom: Religion and America's public schools.* Westport, CN: Praeger.

Thomas, W. H. 1996. *Life worth living: How someone you love can still enjoy life in a nursing home—The Eden alternative in action.* Acton, MA: VanderWyk & Burnham.

Thompson, H. S. 1973. *Fear and loathing on the campaign trail '72.* New York: Warner.

Thompson, W. G. 2005. *The placebo effect and health: Combining science and compassionate care.* Amherst, NY: Prometheus.

Tierney, S. 2004. *Constitutional law and national pluralism.* Oxford, UK: Oxford University Press.

Totally unauthorized guide to Super Street Fighter II. 1994. Indianapolis, IN: Brady.

Trudeau, K. 2004. *Natural cures "they" don't want you to know about.* Elk Grove Village, IL: Alliance.

Turque, B. 2008, November 2. Incentives can make or break students: Ethical issues come with gains on tests. *Washington Post,* p. C01. Retrieved on November 8, 2008 from: http://www.washingtonpost.com/wp-dyn/content/article/2008/11/01/AR2008110101989.html.

Ullrich, D. 2003, April 29. Bikers beware: Motorcycle deaths on the rise. *HealthLink.* Retrieved on September 12, 2008 from: http://healthlink.mcw.edu/article/1031002245.html.

United States Department of Education. 1989. *Rural education: A changing landscape.* Washington, DC: Office of Educational Research and Improvement.

United States Department of Education. 2002. *No child left behind: A desktop reference.* Washington, DC: Author.

United States House of Representatives Committee on Education and the Workforce. 2003. *Head Start: working towards improved results for children: Hearing before the Subcommittee on Education Reform of the Committee on Education and the Workforce, House of Representatives, One Hundred Eighth Congress, first session, hearing held in Washington, DC, March 6, 2003.* Washington, DC: Government Printing Office.

United States Senate Committee on Health, Education, Labor, and Pensions. 2005. *Early education and care: What is the federal government's role? Hearing before the Subcommittee on Education and Early Childhood Development of the Committee on Health, Education, Labor, and Pensions, United States Senate, One Hundred Ninth Congress, first session, on examining the federal role to improve the effectiveness and coordination of childhood education programs, including the Head Start Program, the Child Care and Development Fund, and increasing food security and reducing hunger, April 20, 2005.* Washington, DC: Government Printing Office.

United States Senate Committee on the Judiciary. 1954. *Juvenile delinquency comic books: Hearings before the Subcommittee to Investigate Juvenile*

Delinquency of the Committee on the Judiciary. Washington, DC: Government Printing Office.

Van Ausdale, D., & Feagin, J. R. 2001. *The first R: How children learn race and racism.* Lanham, MD: Rowman & Littlefield.

Vandiver, M. 2006. *Lethal punishment: Lynchings and legal executions in the South.* New Brunswick, NJ: Rutgers University Press.

Wald, M. L. 2007a, July 1. Handlebars: For riders, risk is growing. *New York Times.* Retrieved on May 28, 2009 from: http://query.nytimes.com/gst/fullpage.html ?res=9803E5D6143EF932A35754C0A9619C8B63.

Wald, M. L. 2007b, September 7. Rise in motorcycle deaths renews helmet law. *New York Times.* Retrieved on September 12, 2008 from: http://www.nytimes .com/2007/09/12/us/12helmet.html?_r=1&scp=3&sq=rising%20motorcycle %20deaths&st=cse&oref=slogin.

Webster, C. 2007. *Understanding race and crime.* Berkshire, UK: Open University Press.

Weiss, J. 2003. *The politics of hate: Anti-Semitism, history, and the Holocaust in modern Europe.* Chicago: Ivan Dee.

Wertham, F. 1954. *Seduction of the innocent.* New York: Rinehart.

Westheimer, J. 2007. *Pledging allegiance: The politics of patriotism in America's schools.* New York: Teachers College Press.

What's this thing called brat camp? 2009. *Boot Camps Info.* Retrieved on 5 April, 2009 from: http://www.boot-camps-info.com/brat-camp.html.

Wheeler, A. 2003. *Designing brand identity: A complete guide to creating, building, and maintaining strong brands.* Hoboken, NJ: Wiley.

When "tough love" is too tough. 2007, October, 16. *New York Times.* Retrieved on April 5, 2009 from: http://www.nytimes.com/2007/10/16/opinion/16tue3 .html.

Whitbread, N. 1972. *The evolution of the nursery-infant school: A history of infant and nursery education in Britain, 1800–1970.* London: Routledge & K. Paul.

Whitley, R. 1999. *Divergent capitalisms: The social structuring and change of business systems.* Oxford, UK: Oxford University Press.

Whorton, J. C. 2002. *Nature cures: The history of alternative medicine in America.* Oxford, UK: Oxford University Press.

Wiencek, H. 2003. *An imperfect god: George Washington, his slaves, and the creation of America.* New York: Farrar, Straus, Giroux.

Wilderness camp safety: Putting the risks in perspective. 2009. *Boot Camps Info.* Retrieved on 5 April, 2009 from: http://www.boot-camps-info.com/ wilderness-safety.html.

Wilding, C. 2007. *Emotional intelligence.* Blacklick, OH: McGraw–Hill.

Yaukey, J., & Benincasa, R. 2008, March 26. Motorcycle deaths rose as states rolled back helmet laws. *Gannett News Service.* Retrieved on September 12, 2008 from: http://gns.gannettonline.com/apps/pbcs.dll/article?AID=/20080326/ MOTORCYCLE/803210302.

York, B. 2005. *The vast left wing conspiracy: The untold story of how Democratic operatives, eccentric billionaires, liberal activists, and assorted celebrities tried to bring down a president, and why they'll try even harder next time.* New York: Crown.

Young, M., & Edis, T. 2004. *Why intelligent design fails: A scientific critique of the new creationism.* New Brunswick, NJ: Rutgers University Press.

Zimmerman, J. C. 2000. *Holocaust denial: Demographics, testimonies, and ideologies.* Lanham, MD: University Press of America.

About the Author

Gerard Giordano is a professor at the University of North Florida. He is the author of numerous publications, including nine previous books. His most recent book, *Solving Education's Problems Effectively: A Guide to the Case Method,* was published by Rowman & Littlefield Education.